Once Was Lost

Book Three of In Dante's Wake

Seth Steinzor

Fomite
Burlington, VT

Poems copyright 2021 © Seth Steinzor
Cover Art © Jennifer Gammon
To see more of Jennifer's art,
visit https://squareup.com/store/jennifergammonart/
All rights reserved. No part of this book may be reproduced in any form or by any means without the prior written consent of the publisher, except in the case of brief quotations used in reviews and certain other noncommercial uses permitted by copyright law.
ISBN-13: 978-1-947917-77-4
Library of Congress Control Number: requested
Fomite
58 Peru Street
Burlington, VT 05401
www.fomitepress.co

This book is dedicated to our children's future.

Epigraphs

Oh, what are they doing in heaven today?
The sin and the sorrow are all gone away.
Peace abounds like a river, they say.
So what are they doing there now?
    - Charles Albert Tindley, *What Are They Doing in Heaven Today*

As the true method of knowledge is experiment, the true faculty of knowing must be the faculty which experiences.
    - William Blake, *All Religions Are One*

We live in a plenitude of incommensurable hierarchies...
    - Kwame Anthony Appiah

When all the forces in your organism come into play, then life will begin to play around you as well. You'll see what your eyes are closed to now, and you'll hear what you've never heard. The music of your nerves will begin to play, you'll hear the music of the spheres, and you'll listen to the grass grow. Just wait, there's no hurry. It will come in its own time!
    - Ivan Goncharov, *Oblomov*

Nanabozho's journey first took him toward the rising sun, to the place where the day begins. As he walked, he worried how he would eat, especially as he was already hungry. How would he find his way? He considered the Original Instructions and understood that all the knowledge he needed in order to live was present in the land. His role was not to control or change the world as a human, but to learn from the world how to be human.
    - Robin Wall Kimmerer, *Braiding Sweetgrass*

In these idyllic early months of the Revolution there appeared among the Russian people that intensity of human feeling towards each other which occurs rarely – perhaps not more than once in a century – in the history of any people.
- B. Yelensky, *In the Struggle for Equality*

Omnia mutantur, nihil interit: errat et illinc
huc venit, hinc illuc, et quoslibet occupat artus
spiritus eque feris humana in corpora transit
inque feras noster, nec tempore deperit ullo,
utque novis facilis signatur cera figuris
nec manet ut fuerat nec forma servat eandem,
sed tamen ipsa eadem est, animam sic semper eandem
esse, sed in varias doceo migrare figuras.
- Ovid, *Metamorphoses*, Book XV[1]

Sometimes too I could see that love is a great room with a lot of doors, where we are invited to knock and come in. Though it contains all the world, the sun, moon, and stars, it is so small as to be also in our hearts. It is in the hearts of those who choose to come in. Some do not come in. Some may stay out forever. Some come in together and leave separately. Some come in and stay, until they die, and after. I was in it a long time with Nathan. I am still in it with him. And what about Virgil? Once, we too went in and were together in that room. And now in my tenderness of remembering it all again, I think I am still there with him too. I am there with all the others, most of them gone but some who are still here, who gave me love and called forth love from me. When I number them over, I am

---

[1] "Everything is changed but nothing perishes. The spirit wanders, going hence, thither, coming thence, hither and takes possession of any limbs it pleases. With equal ease it goes from beasts into human bodies and from us into beasts, not in any length of time does it fail. And as wax is easily moulded in new shapes, nor remains as it had been before, nor keeps the same form, but yet is itself the same; so do I teach that the soul is ever the same, but migrates into different shapes." - trans. by C.K. Scott Moncrieff.

surprised how many there are.
    - Wendell Berry, *Hannah Coulter*

In a perfected sexuality shall continuous life be found.
    - Victoria Woodhull

Where were you when I laid the foundations of the earth?
    - God

> *Baruch atah, Adonai Eloheinu, Melech haoloam, shehecheyanu, v'kiymanu, v'higiyanu lazman hazeh.*[2]

---

[2] "Blessed art thou, lord our god, ruler of the universe, who has kept us alive, sustained us, and brought us to this season."

Contents

Bardo	1
Canto I: Access of Light	3
Canto II: Two Bearded Patriarchs	7
Canto III: Partly Occluded Brilliance	12
Canto IV: Sometimes Like a Particle, Sometimes Like a Wave	20
Canto V: The B Side	24
Canto VI: Wearily Down From a Jeep	30
Canto VII: In This, You See Progress?	34
Canto VIII: Venus	42
Canto IX: Water On Parched Soil	49
Canto X: More Schooling	58
Canto XI: Franklin on Eleanor	65
Canto XII: Eleanor on Franklin	70
Canto XIII: The Marriage Of Heaven And Earth	77
Canto XIV: We Are Dawash Of Akhvilli!	84
Canto XV: Building The Workers' Paradise	91
Canto XVI: Sacrament Of My Grandfather	97
Canto XVII: A History Lesson	103
Canto XVIII: Guilty Of Enticing Others Likewise	109
Canto XIX: A Beat Cop	115
Canto XX: Bunky's Tiara	122
Canto XXI: Places My Morality Comes From	128
Canto XXII: The Malakh-Hamoves	134
Canto XXIII: Trembling On The Verge of Becoming	140
Canto XXIV: A Pinpoint Spotlit Moment	151
Canto XXV: The Bird	158

Canto XXVI: Hear Me Roar	163
Canto XXVII: Gentle, Motionless Arms	170
Canto XXVIII: Antiphonal Hymn From the Crystalline Sphere	176
Canto XXIX: If You Want To See It, There It Is	182
Canto XXX: Lushens, Engreening	187
Canto XXXI: In Which We Meet Some Special People	192
Canto XXXII: Nice Shot, Susan!	198
Canto XXXIII: It's Like, You Know, Indescribable	203
Notes on the Text and Sources	211
Acknowledgments	219

Introduction

This is the third and final installment in my retelling of Dante Alighieri's *Commedia*. In *To Join the Lost*, I described a journey through Dante's Hell and the changes wrought there by the seven hundred years ensuing since the visit which he narrated in *L'Inferno*. Also, I observed what has not changed. Despite new denizens, new fashions in old ways of wrong-doing, and misdeeds the saints and sinners of Dante's day could not have imagined or might not have recognized as problematic, the place remains firmly founded in the familiar bedrock of human solipsism and greed.

Among the Lost recounts the trip's second phase. *Il Purgatorio,* the parallel volume in Dante's trilogy, guides us arduously up the Mountain of Purgatory. Its formerly living inhabitants, deprived by death of the capacity to offend god any further, didn't offend god so much when living as to be excluded from paradise, but before they get there, they must tortuously expiate the various injuries their misdirected forms of love have inflicted upon their souls. In the seven hundred years since Dante first visited there, Dante's mountain of faith has been bulldozed flat. A huge, shabby, post-industrial city has grown up on and out of the rubble. *Among the Lost* tours this sad, confused town. Unlike Dante, who was guided as far as the Garden of Eden by the Roman poet Virgil and after that by his lost love Beatrice, I follow Dante's heels all the way to a playing field on the city outskirts, where I encounter Victoria, my own first, lost love.

Finally, paradise. In *Il Paradiso*, having trekked down to Hell's bottom pit and then up the steep slopes and ledges of Purgatory to the undisturbed peace of the Garden of Eden, Dante rockets thence from planet to planet and beyond through the castes of blessedness, until at last he is granted a direct vision of God so powerful that you can't help but believe it even if you don't believe in It. Although the book can be something of a slog for the modern reader due to a dearth of plot development and a surfeit of medieval theology, it's worth it for these final scenes, which fully satisfy Emily Dickinson's famous criterion for great poetry, namely, that it makes you feel as if the top of your head has been blown off.

Some readers of the present book, which carries us by a very different route to a rather different climax, may find themselves wishing to know more about characters and events encountered along the way, or about the sources for certain quotations and assertions. For their convenience, I have appended a Note on the Text and Sources which provides information, canto by canto, that may assuage their curiosity. The book is intended to be readable straight through without this apparatus. Having suffered through the infernal regions and then traversed the twisting streets of the purgatorial city, my guides (now consisting of Dante and a woman who may be either the adult Victoria would have become had she not died, someone else of the same name, or both) and I arrive on a beach. There are fried clams for sale...

Bardo

What I notice when the sun rises
is, I'm hungry. Dumpster diving
fed my slog through Hell but failed to fill the
inner me, and though the trudge through
Purgatory was easier, there I found
only what a man might shove in his
face to keep from feeling empty, hardly
satisfying, even had I
had an appetite. Now I've got one.
Sand grains roll, cool, under the

arches of my feet, between my toes.
When did I take my shoes off?
I don't remember taking off my shoes.
Over there's a tired old school bus,
tireless, axles on cement blocks, a
long, thin, rectangular gash
where its windows used to be, a plywood
shutter raised to shade its length.
Under the gap, shaky red on yellow
drip-fringed brushstrokes announce

C L A M S.

Shouldn't be open this early, but is.
Dawn carries my head's shadow inside.
I say I would like some bellies.
Hip pocket. Wallet. Card: belongs to
someone who might as well be me.
On the paper slip I'm handed, I scrawl the
name the card presents us with.
Off the hot brown mound he shoves on the
counter to me, I pluck a body.

Oh. Oh. The thin crust shatters
'twixt my teeth, gritty shards
freed from the sweet, almost molten flesh.
Into the back of my throat pulses a
tang like extra-sharp cheddar made from iron.
I forget everything else.
Creamy, vegetal visceral mass. Rubbery
anal tube. I chew and swallow.
Parts of me so long neglected praise this
feast; now, I am ready for love.

Canto I: Access of Light

She says, "You may find it helps to keep your
eyes level, loosely focused
on the air a yard or two away, your
jaw relaxed, your spine erect, your
palms up, hands resting on your thighs.
Yes, you're doing it right. Relax.
Are you sitting comfortably? Begin, then.
Take a breath. Now, take another.
Feel it brush the tip of your nose, cool
coming in, and going out it's

warm as you are so you barely feel it
join the ocean of air outside you.
Just that little bit of resistance as the
outside air resists your intrusion.
Here is something you can do. Inhale
gently. Quickly force it out,
huff! huff! huff! huff! huff!
forty times, then let your lungs
do whatever they want, and notice the difference.
Lower your chin when you are full.

Hold it. Feel what it is giving to you;
let it find its own way out,
gently; let it go. Let it go.
You may find when you have learned how
lightly breath can come, you are surprised how
little you really need to live.
That surprise will pass. Don't dwell on it.
Various sounds present themselves. Your
stomach gurgles. Waves roll up the beach,
phssh! phssh! A wire basket

sizzles in oil. The wind strokes your ear.
In the street, an engine rattles.
Each is wrapped in silence. Notice the silence.
Notice your breathing's rhythm. Notice
silence, wrapping each breath like a velvet box.
Am I doing it right, you wonder.
Notice that. I won't tell you.
I am going to let you sit with
all those flywheels spinning in your head.
You have witnessed the depths of human

degradation, the solipsistic pit, the
awful poverty of greed, the
piercing numbness of confusion when the
signs the world abounds with as to
what is right and what is wrong are obscured.
You have balked at the garden gate,
fearing that if you entered it would hurt too
much to leave. Whirr! Whirr!
Maybe it was something someone said to
you at work; it bothered you; at

first you thought you understood, and then you
worried whether you did not.
Maybe it's your mother's ghostly face
peering out of a shop window.
Maybe you're sad. Maybe you're angry. Maybe you
hunger for someone who will lick you, or
where you put your car keys is driving you crazy.
Maybe the greatest puzzle of nature,
question of being, issue of letters, medicine,
law or theology overshadows your

mind like a ship coasting by a quay.
Watch that high, gray hull glide past.
Maybe your left cheekbone sprouts an itch.
Back when I first started trying to
learn to breathe while sitting still, luminous
fringes flickered in the corners
of my vision, and lights like dust motes flaring
in a flashlight beam, but larger,
floated lazily through the room. Once,
dark, smoky tendrils seeped

into my room from under the door, acrid
with a housemate's rage. When I
told my teacher, he laughed and told me not to
worry, 'it's only enlightenment.'
Something, fearing what you're finding, offers
one distraction after another.
Now, remind yourself, 'I'm thinking.' Breathe.
In this body, your breathing holds you
like a mooring cable. That thought you were
carried away with, a boat whose hull is

thinner than a dream, floats away,
leaving you behind. Again, a
passing fancy captures you. 'I'm dreaming,'
you say; on the departing stern in
gold leaf, you read, 'Dreaming.' The barest moment
after it's gone, you're snared again!
Name your captor. Breathe. One day, through the
chinks between those moments you spend
hauled on board your mental boat, dangling
like a swordfish from a mental

yardarm, suddenly you will catch a glimpse of
indescribable amplitude and
freedom. If you maintain this discipline, you'll
see them longer and more often.
Like a baby playing peek-a-boo,
you will learn to trust that they are
still there, even when you do not see them.
You will see your life in them. Your
shadow recedes across each grain of sand. An
empty shell glows pink."

Canto II: Two Bearded Patriarchs

Two bearded patriarchs join us. She greets them:
"Sigmund, it's a joy to see you!
You, too, Karl, as always! Sigmund, stub that
nasty thing, and hug me hello!
Karl, is that a disapproving look?
Silly man! Was it not your
vision – a world recovered from the poison of
gender power games, where healthy
men and women might embrace as merely
wholly human equals? Pardon

me for choosing to live there! Old bourgeois,
you foresaw this bright future
as a byproduct of the stony, grinding
economic dialectic you
dreamed and taught would someday mill us finer.
Blissful hopes that we both shared!
So, embrace me too, Karl! Or am I
just a woman who talks too much?"
"My dear Madam, never were you ever a
woman whom silence would have improved.

Those who thought that, called you Mrs. Satan.
They're all dead, and worse, forgotten.
I knew what to make of you no more than
nearly anyone else. Such words!
'Frivolous crackpot humbug rich man's tool' -
this I called you. Crazy American,
maybe across so much water I could
not discern your true dimensions.
Gripped by Ideas, I didn't care to look.
I was seized by the notion I had

seized upon history's motive force. Bah!
Contradictions of capital? Bah!
Blinded by ink, I overlooked so much my
wife and daughters may have taught me,
had I the wit, of the world's ground plan.
You were focused on the ends my
focus on the means left me no time for.
Only towards the end of my works,
musing on archaeology, had I an inkling:
fragments freed from centuries of

grit evidenced potentialities
for the sexes far other than
our era's sorry and rigid relations.
We were eating the same sausage:
I, from one end; from the other, you.
To be fair to me, that person
so strange to our times: that person who could
walk beyond oppression; who could
live on fruits of actions so belonging
to all those with whom she communed that

our word 'labor' with its sour odor of
misappropriation no longer
can describe such freely productive relations;
who, not alienated, flowers;
I could not imagine that in you she
lived, generations early."
"Mr. Marx, you say the sweetest things!
Sweeter still, it's not mere sweet talk,
though you give me too much credit. Brave new
world, had it such people in it!

Sigmund, were you listening?" "Always I listen.
Who, may I ask, is your quiet friend?
All we know of him is that he's breathing.
From that, much may be deduced, but...
Does he come to meet us with a purpose?"
"Yes!" But after that exclamation,
nothing. I stifle an urge to fill the gap,
interested in their accounts of themselves
more than in whatever they may say of the
transcendental vision towards which

I am sure that she and Dante lead me.
Freud says, "Good. Welcome to the
heaven of broken promises: everyone's heaven.
Our friend Mr. Marx confesses
how the open book he thought to make of
history's hidden mainspring is missing
at least half its pages. As are mine. The
data of my eyes and ears, the
data lodged behind them, I dismissed like
unappreciated servants.

All those miseries my first patients brought in
hopes that by the magic of my
listening I might elicit from them the Names which,
uttered, would vanish their symptoms – poof!
In the awe and excitement of that morning
of discovery, when I sought the
fons et origo of mental disorders
in my patients' words, as no one
had before except my mentor Breuer,
I was amazed and bemused how nearly

all of them relived on the couch the pain of
elders interfering with them.
You know what I mean, my dear." "My father
made me a woman before my time."
"Just so. It shocked me into belief.
I had found the sovereign key! Or
so I thought. For I'd seen how Naming cures.
But, although this was a Name of
such undoubted power it could not be
spoken aloud in public, yet it

failed to release their symptoms from my patients.
Here my hubris hobbled me:
if the lock stuck shut for me, the doctor!
then the fault was in the key.
I did not consider that the patient
was the one who had to turn it.
No, I found a plethora of reasons
now to doubt what I'd thought certain.
How could perversion have undone so many?
If my siblings showed some symptoms –

I, myself! – must I accept the horrid
inference of our father's guilt?
Lost in the shadows, the memory of a maid in my
father's house, the thick folds
where her bulging thighs joined, the used and
reddish waters in which she bathed me.
Fleeing from the implications, I spun a
web of polymorphous perversity,
psychosexual development, Oedipus complex,
ego, id, and superego,

strong enough to bear me far, indeed,
strong enough to become my prison."
I say, "When the mists of religion parted,
you ground lenses we still use to
scope out what was hidden behind them." Marx says,
"Cracked," and Freud says, "Wrong prescription.
Had I but kept faith with what I knew..."
She says, "Boys, don't get all mopey.
It's so easy, here, beyond survival,
to forget that struggling animal,

steps removed from the all-but-wordless apes,
barely able to read its own face,
you! – conscious of less than you were aware of,
understanding less than that.
Charlie Darwin – where is he? – would school you.
We did pretty well for critters
bred to elude the tigers long enough to
eat a banana and raise a child.
Even in heaven, only buddhas know all they
know." Exeunt the boys, whistling.

Canto III: Partly Occluded Brilliance

"What did you mean when you said your father made you...
Did you mean what I think you meant?
Oh, I am so sorry!" "Did I say that?
So I did. And if my pa
made me a woman before my time, by adding
sexual uses to the household
drudgery poor frontier female children like
me were born to, why say, 'Sorry'?
You didn't do it. I learned so much from him!
That man taught me in the plainest

and most vigorous terms just what sex is when
sex is wholly in man's dominion.
If the price of that knowledge was to suffer,
it was the cost of a woman's schooling.
I am not diminished by having sorrowed.
Damn that man for being willing
to exact such pain. Damn him for being
willing I should be the one who
paid to scratch his itch. Damn him for being
no better than a sickly

wife who bore ten children to him, and the
six who survived, could force him to be.
Hell is where he skulks. But, pity me not!"
Lips firm, defiant eyes
glaring, arms folded across her breasts, she
laughs. "That is a pose I liked to
strike, when I gave my inspiring speeches,
just before I'd evoke their pity on
me for being so brave and solitary; but
you, who draw one breath at a time, will

want to know in proper chronological
order how I came to join the
congregation whose partly occluded brilliance
lights this humble corner of heaven.
I hope it will be your future home!
Don't be abashed by those two lusters
you just met: you might meet almost anyone
here, among the bulbs that flickered.
I'll confess I've found here few who shared with
me the muddy desolation

of my birthplace, but perhaps they all lived
up to whatever their promise was.
Mine being more extravagant, I failed.
I spoke its first syllables from on
top of a stump, haranguing the other children as
long as I could keep them thronging
down there on the dirt among the chickens.
Each of the revival preachers
who'd most recently whipped our elders into the
sex-fired frenzies of true religion

tutored me unwittingly how to do it.
'Lord have mercy on you all!' I'd
holler at the first to shift their eyes from
five-year-old me. 'Hellfire's a'comin'!'
That would hold them just a little longer.
I could talk you into the ground,
telling you all I learned, as time went by, of
grabbing crowds and holding them. But
life is a braid of many strands, and this one
I will leave unstrung in the telling.

You have not come all this way for me to
teach you such tricks, worthy of monkeys
striving to rule the tribe's attention. I'll say,
I was a masterful monkey mistress!
That came later, after I had clawed my
way free of my family's uses.
This I managed by finding myself a man, or
I should say letting him find me, or
guiding him by none too subtle hints to
where I was waiting, the spidery means a

female of my station might avail to
leave her home with her rep if not her
hymen intact. Choices. I chose me a
gentle, well-spoken drunk. His
morphine addiction came later. He was all my
purposes needed, so I thought. I
even thought I loved him! That illusion
died the night I bore our baby
on our apartment's bare plank floor,
while my medically licensed husband

snored on the couch in stupor; a 'love' replaced, I
add, in that same instant by a
larger love for these two helpless creatures,
one fallen the other delivered
into helplessness, the first who taught me
gentle manners and how to swim in
social waters, the second who rode my waters
into a social world he'd never
learn to navigate without me, being
feeble of body and weak of mind. The

other love, that should inspire and inform
procreation but so disastrously
my son's father had no strength to give me,
came to me not much later. He was
tall, bearded, a wounded warrior. He'd led
thousands of men through days of battle
and the weeks and months of toil between them,
helplessly watching his boys fall to
illness more than to the enemy's lead that
pierced so many. I told him that

spirit voices spoke in my nerves daily.
He said this was part of my beauty,
also, my prelapsarian sexual attitudes.
'Prelapsarian' was his word. He
taught me words; his profit was, I taught him
what was meant by 'prelapsarian.'
Those were golden days! Love and nothing
else determined our bond.
Oh, so many strands I leave unwoven!
Hear, I'm talking to you about love, with

never a word of my daughter, my joy, her father's
gift. He wept as if relieved to
see her light break upon his remorse.
That was before I met the Colonel.
He was fighting and learning to doubt the worth of
most of what he was fighting for.
When I tell you love and nothing else was our
lodestar and our faith's foundation,
you may underestimate the ferocious
desperation of our creed."

"I grew up in the 'sixties. By the time I
turned eighteen, in nineteen seventy,
it was clear to me that Uncle Sam
wanted me to kill or be killed
for a lie. Now that good ol' boy,
Dubya, him of the fake ranch and
fake military service and fake
weapons of mass destruction and fake
coalition of the falsely willing, is
riding high on the death machine."

"Well, you may have some small notion."
Sharers of inklings, we smile. She says,
"How I rose to prominence is the usual
tangle of luck, connections, alignment of
personal qualities with the times' proclivities,
perseverance, strength of faith in
all the above, myself, and my advisers, not
all of whom were in the flesh. It
helped to possess a form that sparked desire, and
that the things I had to say were true.

One great plutocrat whom my voices charmed
set me up as a Wall Street broker.
In return, I brought him intelligence of the
men who sought my ear in lieu of
other parts. Encouraged, the Colonel and I
sought to speak to wider spheres.
We collected a circle of politicians,
preachers, sages, leaders, disciples.
Men dictated the words, that I gave meaning.
Later, I found words of my own.

I taught: women equal men in
reason, intelligence, depth and breadth of
soul and vision, and forensic acumen;
for example, I offered myself.
I taught: women as well as men by
birthright are entitled to all the
rights and responsibilities of a citizen;
for example, I offered myself.
I taught: marriage without love is
prostitution, so not to despise

painted ladies, theirs being the common lot.
I taught: sex is natural,
shameless as breathing, if love is its inspiration.
I taught: neither by law nor
custom nor oath can anyone own my love, that
it is not bestowed for eternity,
I may change it without let or hindrance.
I taught: lack of parental
love deforms children. I taught:
those who live and the lost to life are

no more separated than are
man from woman and rich from poor and
ours from all the other races we could
hear and learn from, if we'd listen.
I taught: no one has justice
until every one oppressed by
reason of race, gender, or class has justice, and
not 'til then will that old dream of
government of, by, and for the people
have been born upon this earth.

For example of each, I offered myself.
Audiences ate it up; but,
what they heard was, I had sex a lot.
You may laugh! But, tell me, please,
one hundred forty years later,
how much have our countrymen learned? It
seems they well absorbed what may be used to
justify self-gratification."
Long silence. I study the ground. I say,
"Love is a harder lesson, I guess."

"Hearing, they did not listen; not having listened, they
could not hear. They gave their meanings
to my words. I really can't complain! My
fall from popular grace was the usual
tangle of miscalculation, bad luck, and
pigeons that had grown into buzzards
coming home to roost. One of my sisters
blackmailed our mutual benefactor.
Failing to appreciate her faithfulness
to her father's values, he severed

all relations. Rumors of my evil
promiscuity spread, and of my
gutter-spawned threat to the roots of social order.
I recruited defenders by threatening
powerful men's hypocrisy with exposure.
Poor tactics, to fight on their field.
They struck first! My repudiation by
Mr. Marx was the least of my worries.
I would have fought on, but I had
offered up others in my stead, so

I had surrendered the strength that came from being
my example. Health failing,
I abandoned the Colonel and found a man who
loved me more than what I stood for.
He transported me far away from the battle.
Living anew in Olde England, I
learned to save my striving not for mankind,
rather by modest and persevering
measures to alleviate those parts of it
I could circle with my arms."

Canto IV: Sometimes Like a Particle, Sometimes Like a Wave

"Dante," I say, "Are you still with us?
Speak up! What is this place?
Does it look to you like heaven?" Dante:
"Heaven revealed Itself to my senses,
they being my only means to perceive It.
This may just as well be It as
that translucent sphere I saw with faces
surfacing in It like fish in a pond."
Gulls' creaky cries. Briny, sweet.
Warmth behind, coolth ahead.

"Is that, then, the poets' broken promise,
to describe the indescribable?"
I ask. He says, "Whitman claims 'the unseen is
proved by the seen, 'till that becomes
unseen and receives proof in its turn.'"
"'Yesterday, upon the stair, I
met a man who wasn't there,'" I sing.
She says, "Do your job and even
prosy folk like me will feel precisely
what you're going on about."

I say, "You, Miz Prosy Enigma, failed to
mention teaching meditation
in the histoire of your repertoire.
Where, among the smoke-filled rooms and
lecture halls, did you pick that up?" She says,
"I will have you know, sir,
in my place of business, we required the
gents to take their cigars outside. But,
as to what you ask, I am at a
loss to answer, being torn and

undecided as a mule between two
equal sacks of grain and needing
just the faintest nudge from somewhere to help me.
On the one hand, I'm a plain girl
from Ohio given to speaking her mind,
gifted with words but not with the power to
point behind them. But I'm loathe to ask a
man, once more, to lend his words to
hold my meaning." Dante: "Beautiful eloquent
lady, I found God through watching the

eyes of a woman, attending to where she looked, and
looking there. May it please you,
I would gladly give you voice." She nods.
"So, I turn to our young friend.
You are living in this world; your life is
in you, like a braided river
lacing a floodplain with its skein of channels.
In its waters, there you swim.
Some of the islands stay dry in every season.
Some of the banks are never drowned.

You may float at the current's whim, sometimes
placidly, sometimes in confusion where
tendencies tangle, sometimes in rapids' uproar.
You may choose to ride the surface,
playing in the play of light and dark, or
you may choose to ply deeper.
You may choose to expend the effort of leaving
one current for another,
or, with greater effort still, the channel
towards which you are being borne

for another, newly cut perhaps in
last month's torrential rains.
You may choose to speed downstream, or, risking
quicker and possibly fatal exhaustion, to
turn against the unremitting urge, or
even to paddle from side to side,
angling across the waters' press to keep your
bearing on this tree, that boulder.
Sometimes, you may find, in the briefest fragment
of a flashing instant, that you have

risen out of the flux, up the bank to
where you were not built to live, and,
in that unaccustomed, rarefied medium,
rest, the burdens of daily being
eased. In that single flash or glint, the
whole riverine embroidery
bursts upon your eye, piping its landscape
under the sun and the other stars: your
farthest departure from your course and also
summons back to it that instant.

When at last, as worn out as a salmon
that's come home, you surrender,
all of this will spread in silver sheets and
be absorbed and disappear
into the rich alluvial soils that held its
threads distinct until their spate.
If you follow the figure of my speech,
it should come quite clear to you how
she, having passed that final filter,
may teach you to stand upon it."

I direct my words past him to her.
"I am thinking how an infant's
fingers wrapped the smallest one of mine.
In that tiny grasp was promise
more than anyone can keep! This heaven
of the fallen short, is it merely
that same world which all of us were born to?
Why are you smiling?" Why is she looking
at me like a lover, after love, with
almost painfully shining eyes?

Canto V: The B Side

She says, "Poet, speak for me again."
Dante: "When the earth's face
greets the sun, receiving that which tenders
life's potentials, who rejoices?"
She says, "Being understood is joyful."
I say, "If I understood you
any better, you might burn me up!"
He says, "Toasted, but not consumed!
Step into the flames, my son."   "You say my
life's in me, and I'm in it?

Well, okay, I guess. But, it's got many
branches, besides the one I'm in?
I don't get it!" Yes, her eyes grow brighter.
He says, "In your physics, every
possible path from A to B is where you
might observe an entity moving
through those points, or all of them at once. The
quantum physicists swaddle this theory
in the ugliest appellation:
'path integral formulation.'

See the rhyme I made? Just as *piccolo*
rhymes so deeply with *ridicolo*.
Think how God, whom you prefer to label
'Nature' or some such euphemism,
builds with parsimonious architectonics
infinitely varied forms:
how a tree, its roots and trunk and branches,
patterns the neuron that beholds it
and the lightning bolt that blasts them both;
how the fearsome tidal eddy

turns in your blood to flap your heart's valves;
how the nautilus shell's whorl
purrs like the ocean and holds the galaxy's arms.
Why, then, should you find it strange that the
vanishingly small abounds in rhymes with the
dream through which your selves daily
ride their body along its brute paths?
Bear in mind that metaphors' meanings
lose coherence just when they approach most
closely the inexpressibly true;

also, remember that every word is a metaphor."
Now he launches an extended –
what else can I call it but a rant? It's
burden is the burden of choice,
how the guilt-ridden twenty-first century,
"using your science to blinker your vision,
labels illusory your most precious asset."
I say, "All this iron insistence
on free will! You bound your morality to it
so tightly, no wiggle

room and only one choice on offer,
right or wrong, and no excuses.
You remind me of tales of brave Ulysses, who
lashed himself to the mast, as the song goes,
'how his naked ears were tortured by the
sirens sweetly singing'." She breathes,
"Oh, I love that tune." "What seductive
hymns tormented you, old mentor?"
"It is hinted at throughout my books."
"All the world's between your lines!

Knowing that a poet means to serve his
work by writing about his life, and
not the other way around, I don't think
more than half of you is hid there.
I would like to read you more directly.
Honor me by listening to your
story as I understand it, as it
has been handed on to me.
I am thinking of that horrible year your
father died, ripping a hole in the

world, and she in whom you had reposed
all your love, your Beatrice,
fell into that same abyss, and into
politics you plunged, headlong
off the high board, hoping to drown.
But, you did not sink, you swam.
You were wicked smart, good-hearted, gifted with
psychological x-ray vision,
wisdom, social grace, the art of framing
words for almost any occasion.

Don't blush. And, did I say well-read?
You could top them, always! – with a
line from someone else, if not your own.
So, the top is where you rose to.
Showering all those gifts, before too long your
counsel was essential. Nothing in
Florentine civic affairs passed without you
first pronouncing on it, and with your
voice weighing heavily in the balance.
Who said poets are *un*acknowledged

legislators? That poor man was salving
his own fecklessness with a phrase.
You were right in the heart of things, working with
words, working things with your words.
Just like Vaclav Havel –" "Yes, I've met him."
"Oh, to have bugged that conversation!"
"What is there to say? Had you carried a
sword at Campaldino, we might
nod to each other, veterans sharing secrets by
virtue of common experiences.

So, with Havel... we clink glasses... sigh... "
"What you found, when you had dived as
deep as if you were fishing for coins or pearls, was a
mess of families squabbling for dominance.
Being as we're the wordy animal, it was
always in the name of something:
god, of course; pope; emperor; Guelph;
Ghibelline; White; Black; et
cetera to the end of our time in the world.
Tussles in alleys. Cold looks.

In Pistoia, a child throws a snowball. From
where it strikes drip years of bloodshed."
"*Si, ricordo*. He was a Cancellieri. His
uncle, laughing, chastised him, for
which the little boy, a few days later,
dared to form his fingers fist-like and
swipe it at the uncle. For which, the boy's
cousin, Focaccia, cut his hands off.
Then Focaccia slew the uncle, his father; and
over this murder, all Pistoia –"

"Men," she says. He says, "Fought. At last,
we of Firenze marched in, severed their
leaders from their factions, and caught from them the
slowly fatal inflammation,
to which we were too much predisposed. It
spread like consumption – Cerchi, Donati..."
"May I direct the witness' attention to the
year the infection came to a head in
your fair city? You, a Cerchi-ist from a
clan of Whites, your wife a Donati

Black; freshly installed in the highest office, you
tried to preserve the Florentine peace by
what had seemed to work in Pistoia: exile.
Your wife's cousins. Your best friend. You
must have felt the agony of a wolf who
gnaws its leg to escape a trap.
One year later, the parties you had pissed off
hammered you back, on that phantom limb, and
you were exiled. Pain demands answers. You, like
Job, interrogated justice." The

light is growing, as if from without and within.
    "But there was that other song the
maimed sing to the maimed, the lost to the lost.
You could hear it all too well.
It is the anthem of those who belong to nothing
but each other. The moon sings it.
His Holiness the Dalai Lama
calls it compassion. It is love that
neither pities nor hopes. Namaste!
That's your canticle's B side."

Canto VI: Wearily Down From a Jeep

When they crank the rheostat fully up, the
speck of dust the cleaner missed
on the chandelier goes woozy with dazzlement.
That's how I feel. "Keep your head down,"
she says, "Rest it on my lap. You've been
overwhelmed by our delight in
you. Easy, easy. You are not the
first whose hair I've stroked through sickness.
He was sweating out booze and dope, but you are
suffering from a sweeter surfeit.

Listen: may I soothe you with a story?" She
reads my nod of assent with her thighs.
"It will be a story told in pictures.
Moving pictures. I love the movies!"
At this point, her lips project no sounds, but
images play inside my head.
First: *a great tree. An ape sits*
nearly atop it, far out on a
brawny, twisted branch, beneath a sparse,
oval canopy of leaves,

*gazing over tawny grasslands, marveling
at a murmuration of starlings
that elongates, condenses, contracts, folds,
falls, balloons, rises, circles,
smoothly blobulating in wordless unison.*
Next: *a baby ape, mouth open,
belly heaving. The other seventeen are
scattered throughout the clearing: a couple
up in trees, looking out; a half a
dozen youngsters rough and tumbling;*

*pairs of adults taking turns picking
ticks and fleas and lice to eat (no
wastage); singletons combing the grass for nuts. An
adolescent male leaves off
whacking a rock with a stick, and cuddles the baby.
From the lookouts, alarm: aliens! The
adolescent male retrieves his stick.*
Next: *black chicks' gaping
mouths greet snowy parent returning full of
fish from the world's heaving belly*

*to the dimpled cliffs and headlands. She
zeros in on the nine square feet she
low-pitched caw caw calls her own. Her
mate extends his golden neck. They
clack beaks. A neighbor encroaches, is fiercely
warned away. Tens of thousands such
families inhabit this sea-side colony, each in its
self-policed, invisible cell, more
regular than swarming honeycomb.*
"It's an anarchist's dream!" I exclaim.

She says, "Social life without society."
Next: *outside the forest, a patch of
bare earth, dotted with small mounds
from which seedlings poke their wrinkle-
folded leaflets. Surrounding grasses' shadows
stretch to touch them, almost. In their
trees, the lookouts tensely scan the clumps of
lemongrass, red oat, rhodes and
elephant grass for anomalous tawny knots
creeping contra the evening's breeze; it's*

*nearly the hour the cats begin to prowl.
All clear. Safe to go home.
Shouldering hoes, the weary gardeners gather in
bunches around the plot's perimeter
while the lookouts descend and reclaim their spears.
Proof against dusk's enmity,
they depart for their respective villages.*
Next: *the ring of the horizon,
viewed from a tower on the ring of the city's walls.
In the afternoon's light and heat, his*

*bald pate gleams like a cabochon.
"I know how you feel," he says to his
young companion, "Both our fathers came here
due to drought and bandits elsewhere."*
Next: *beneath the wall, a crone of fifty
and a girl on the verge of menarche
tend to dyeing vats. "But grandma, why?" the
girl asks, poking the fire with a stick.
"When the outsiders pierce our defenses and enter the
town, they rape because it makes our*

men feel bad, so they feel good," she answers.
Next: *beneath a tree, a man
talks to a crowd about the gap desire
opens between themselves and happiness,
each of us the same, and how to close it.
Deer nibble the lawn nearby.*
Next, in rapid succession: *the Kabah, a whirlpool of
white-robed pilgrims flowing around it.
Splashing spread-eagled into the ocean off a
schooner, a black body. A grinning

limey hugs a grass-skirted, bare-breasted woman.
Men in silken robes and tailored
woolen three-piece suits raise a
toast around a walnut table.
Grimy-faced miners, picketing. Two women
chain themselves to a fence. Two
soldiers huddle together, shivering in a
muddy foxhole. A huge room,
full of women polishing metal cones.
People tumble from cattle cars. A

rusty ship, its deck jammed with ragged
people of all ages staring
anxiously at an approaching pilot boat.
Men in white coats staring
at a small, round, glass dish a
white-coated woman holds before them.
In the clear sky, a single airplane;
suddenly, to the morning sun a
sun is added. Blue-helmeted soldiers
climb wearily down from a jeep.*

Canto VII: In This, You See Progress?

Freezing on a closeup of haunted eyes
peering from under a blue shell, the
pictures stop. She says, "In a millenium,
humans may love humans, as such."
Standing next to her, a bearded gentleman,
who was not beside her before,
shakes his head. "Don't be so sure," he says.
She says, "May I introduce you
to each other, my dear Seth and Charlie?"
He says, "Pleased to meet you, young man."

I say, "If you are the author of that
book whose closing paragraph starts by
meditating, 'It is interesting to
contemplate an entangled bank, with
many plants', and if, in writing, style is a
function of the substance conveyed, then
you have written the most elegantly
beautiful prose I've ever read, and the
honor of this encounter, sir, is most
definitely completely mine."

He says, "Thank you for your gratifying
praise. I hardly expected, in my own
lifetime, for my work, or, once my work was
known to the public, my poor self, to
be so fulsomely greeted. But, to the point.
One effect my work accomplished
was the total if grudging eradication of
teleology from biology.
That most certainly was not my intent;
though, a prettier argument for

that conclusion would be hard to conceive.
Most enchanted to see you, madam,
and your friends. If you will excuse me,
I must go and play with my children."
I say, "Something in me balks at 'millennium.'
Eyes open. Hearts change.
Five of Gautama's buddies, who'd studied with him
in the school of self-denial,
but, unable to stomach his moderation,
broke with him, disgusted, met him

on the road by happenstance years later,
listened with full attention to his
fully articulated teachings, heard him
well, and donned the saffron robes.
Constantine flipped the Roman Empire to Christ.
Here I am, talking with people
no one else can see, on a beach that no one
else perceives is paradise,
maybe except that girl in the blue bikini
all blissed out from yoga class – it's

something in the way she moves – and just last
week I would have called me crazy."
Someone in the distance (perhaps it's Marx) says,
"Two hundred years ago, for
freedom your fantasy precondition was, the
last king to be strangled in the
last priest's guts. Now you say the
last *oligarch* in the last
fundamentalist's viscera to be strangled.
In this, you see progress?" She says,

"Charlie, help us." Darwin, with some reluctance:
"I suppose the children can wait.
You must consider where you come from and are
not so very far removed from,
in the infancy of our species. I shall
spare you a discourse upon your
earliest ancestors' material culture, and
rest content with pointing out the
relative cushion your condition of life
interposes against the razor-thin

margin they by dint of daily struggle
balanced their existence upon.
Pumping stations bring you water cleansed of
harmful creatures and noxious substances,
to imbibe beneath a well-sheathed roof.
In your closet, you may select from a
range of habiliments suitable to the various
social occasions and states of weather
likely for you to encounter. Foodstuffs adequate
to maintain your being in a

tolerable state of health and daily activity
are reliably to be procured at
any of a number of locations
more or less convenient to you.
Medical science alleviates your suffering,
often providing also a cure.
Lack of any of these you count as but a
step away from the direst poverty.
Your progenitors lacked not one, but all.
Prone to broken bones, contusions,

lacerations, tooth decay, and all the
other avenues of morbidity,
they relieved their thirst, exposure, nudity,
hunger, and ailments with whatever
nature presented to hand within walking distance.
Meager trade supplied some needs.
Crying, a baby in the night was a beacon
for the delectation of larger
predators: bear-sized hyenas, saber-toothed cats.
All a lifetime's passions confined, with the

lesser emotions and sentiments too, among a
few dozen mostly consanguine
individuals who comprised their social
world in its near entirety, a
gene pool refreshed just often enough to
reinvigorate the stock, or
doomed by isolation to enfeeblement.
This mode of existence sufficed you
comfortably enough, however precarious,
nearly all the time since when you

first emerged a species distinct from that which
birthed bonobos, chimps, and you,
up to the present moment; some millions of years.
You must acknowledge, a concomitant
of a lifestyle so constrained the wages of
any choice could well be death, would
be an inclination to conservatism
highly pronounced in thought and deed.
Natural selection, as we know, proceeds by
tiny changes accumulated

slowly, from generation to generation.
'Natura non facit saltum.'
Starting from such as this, and differing from your
hairy siblings more in technical
forms of intelligence than in social skill,
should it surprise you that long after
anatomically modern humanity burst into
being, you remain a creature
savagely preferential to your tribe?
Variations better endowed to

calculate risk, perforce less averse to it,
spread across the globe and improved your
handiness with stone, and fire, and bone, and
wood, and other flora, supplanting
those less usefully deft or killing them off.
In this connection I should mention, if
only for the purpose of disavowal,
that pernicious doctrine with which my
name is applauded in certain precincts of hell.
Of the notion biology justifies

economic or social injustice, I say,
nature has planted in your core the
noble faculty of regard for your kind.
Some might choose to set this aside for
purposes of their own, and breed you like dogs or
pigeons or maize, culling the weak and – "
Interrupting, Victoria: "I, naively and
thoughtlessly, in revulsion against the
labor and pain of unassisted caring for
my disabled son, and to my

shame, in contradiction to my heart's own
witness for love and freedom, turning my
heart against my heart, allowed myself to
lend my voice to the cause of eugenics."
He continues, "With respect, ma'am,
may I clarify, for the sake of
your young protegé, whose expression
evidences shock in the very
highest degree, this is not a heaven
where no sin, nor the memory of it, is

granted admittance. Nothing is unmixed,
here like anywhere; there's no perfect
finch, capable of outcompeting all in
every environmental niche;
never a nec plus ultra; no-one free from
conflict or failure. As I was saying:
Nature's improvisations being unplanned, She
offers no example of trading
off a trait of past and proven worth for
future hypothesized improvement; but

adaptation by self-mutilation
is a common psychopathology.
Those who'd practice such husbandry should consider the
insult to which it would expose their
organs of conscience. Possibly damage may be
minimized by minimizing the
breeding program's number of generations.
Even so, one might expect to
see disuse incur some atrophy,
possibly novel forms of heartlessness.

Leave it at that. Contemplate instead
how offended compassion sounds,
as you heard just now from the better half of
our most lovely and charming companion, a
tocsin against risks inconceivable
when you first diverged from the apes in
small bands roving and intermittently
brushing up against each other.
Those conditions continued unchanged until
persons better disposed to exceed their

settled habits accrued advantage. Explosive
population and geographic
growth forcibly broadened your notions of kindred:
class, race, religion, community,
workplace, sports club, political party, language,
nation, ethnic homeland, culture,
gender, demographic cohort, preferences.
Mr. Vonnegut's comic coinage
'granfalloon' is strikingly apposite to the
ever expanding webs of affinities

that you have no choice but to navigate, that
finally have enmeshed the globe.
It may fairly be conjectured, whether,
under such conditions, those more
greatly possessed of the higher social functions
gain a reproductive advantage
over more atavistic modes of survival, and
what influence local factors – "
"Like I said, humans may love humans!
Stop 'splaining, Charlie," she says.

Canto VIII: Venus

Tilting back her head, she laughs, her throat's
pale column a fountain of laughter.
I had risen when Darwin began to speak, and
now the brilliant whites of her eyes
and their merry blue catapult my
spirits further upward. She says,
"What are you looking at, my frisky boy?" and
laughs again, and I laugh, too.
Dante: "When I was young, I wrote my wing man
Guido Cavalcanti a sonnet:

Guido, I wish that you and I and our good friend
Lapo were magically whisked to a boat that would
sail wherever we chose to go, regardless
of the wind's direction or strength,
unimpeded by storms or foul weather
over the ocean, and our gift for
being together would grow into ever increasing
appetite for living together.
And, that same good magic should bring aboard our
fine friends Vanna and Lagia

*and that woman who lives at number thirty: and
all the time we'd talk about love, and
each one of them would be happy, as I am
sure each one of us would be.*
Is that not what we are doing, now?
Wonderful dream of heaven, come true!"
She: "That woman who lives at number thirty?"
He: "I said that I was young!"
She: "So, blame it on youth? But I've known plenty of
older men, and women, too, who

could not think of love without they put it
in a carnal frame. Not that
I hold anything against carnality!
But, when coming from a man, it
smacks a tad of the 'massa' crying up the
virtue of loyal service." And Dante:
"That's the kind of thing that Vanna would say,
after her second goblet of wine. But,
if we're going to enter my dream, we'll need at
least another person." I say,

stupidly, "That girl in the blue bikini could
stand in for the woman who lived at
number 30. Wait, what's that?!" A naked
figure wildly waving glow sticks
bright enough to outglare the morning sunrise
hurtles to us all the way from the
distant other end of the beaches as fast as
I can say this, and stops stock still.
Not panting. Not breathing. Victoria
is the first to regain her composure.

She says, "Do we know you, sir?" He answers,
"By what others have made of my works.
By what others have made of my words, dear sister.
By my words, perhaps." That voice! I
know its hiss and ring. From where, I wonder?
Dante: "First having met you, Master,
in the trench of flames, it bewilders my young
friend to see you now ungarbed and
joyful, dancing on the margin of air and
water and earth. May it please you,

teach him a name by which he now might love you."
"That would be the same you harshly
execrated, there, in the Hopeless City.
Rise from your knee. We're friends, here.
Your vituperation was so justly
merited by what I once taught the
nascent church I served concerning women
and their proper place in it, I
cannot help but love you for it now."
I say, "Paul?! The apostle? I'm boggled!

How is it that being there, you're here?"
Dante: "You might better be answered
were you to unpack your confusion and lay it
out before you like a sidewalk
vendor's wares, and not compactly jumbled."
I say, "You taught women to leave their
voices at the meeting-house door, like umbrellas.
'Woman's head is man,' you taught.
Here you crash a party led by a woman
famous for using her voice, and a man who

followed the eyes of his Beatrice to heaven."
"Guilty as charged," he says, "and yet, I
also taught of love." "Yes," I say, "but
not of love between man and woman.
As among brothers and sisters of your faith,
you gave love the place of honor.
When it came to the sexes, I mean as such,
love left your vocabulary.
Then it was, 'I would prefer you don't have
sex, but if you must, get married.'"

She says, "All that hatred of the body.
All that juxtaposing to the
physical what you liked to label 'reason'
as if reason were opposed to
its own heart and hands and guts and genitals."
"Not exactly sex positive,"
says the girl in the blue bikini. He says,
"Guilty, if not quite as charged.
Back before my being was evicted
without cause from the humble home of

meat and bones my parents lovingly made but
Caesar wanted me out of, I was a
teacher and community organizer.
Pride and anger belong to the flesh, so
you will have no cause to suspect me of either
when I say those early converts
could be dumb as rocks; and I have seen a
man pelted to death with stones, so
I know what it means to be hard and wounding.
After a year and a half among them,

I left Corinth only to hear it reported the
congregation I'd founded there was
riven by half a dozen factions, each
claiming sole possession of truth
in the name of one or another of we
several who had taught them, all from the
same syllabus, that one death unites us.
Acting just like Greeks, you might say."
"Or Italians." "We had hoped to make them
different, with our words and passion.

Words and passion! Feeble tools for change,
as you poets know so well."
Looking to Dante and seeing his rueful nod,
I ruefully nod as well, and
fold my arms, frowning, like Victoria.
"Words and passion were all I had.
Quarrels cloaked in religious garb were no less
vicious in those days than now, and
mortal to an infant community, tearing
at itself, hand against hand.

Oh, those stupid, backsliding Corinthians! Preach them
love, I thought, with all the power
in me, and if that is not enough, then
so be it: but, be careful.
Having taken so shaky a grasp on the faith I'd
taught them, they might slide back further
into an abyss of error if I
were to nudge them ever so slightly
clumsily in the wrong direction, give them
knowledge easily misunderstood.

In those days, the secret cults of sex
flourished widely in caves and groves,
led by women, using men as tools of
wine-soaked goddess worship. I was
desperate that those numbskulls learn to love;
but, I feared as much what they might
make of love, through thinking with their dicks.
So, constrained by fear of the greatest
manifestation of creative force and
joy that humans are given to know –

ha! ha! oh, to laugh or to cry –
I presumed to teach them harmony!
Catapulting words and passion at them
from my distance, by epistle,
funny thing: it worked, so far as it went;
men brotherly loving men
in that congregation, for a while."
V. says, "May we understand your
'manifestation' includes gestation and childbirth
in addition to joy, etcetera?"

"They were not in my mind, then," he confesses,
"unlike when I spoke just now.
Who in heaven would deny the sacred
female rite of parturition?
But, you ask me how I came to be here.
It is an irony that I love, as a
lifelong lover of irony, how I came to
heaven riding on those words I
wrote commending love to those Corinthians
and describing it so they could

not mistake it. Even though I shaved and
cleaned its hair and smell and moisture,
my depiction truly was its likeness.
Sweetest of ironies, brothers and sisters:
those words, framed to float above the
question between man and woman
so far no such question could be seen,
are most often intoned, invoking
sentimental tears, at weddings! And they
state a standard for relations

that, had all who've heard it truly listened,
might have saved a world of pain.
People cling to words but forget what's in them,
eat the wrappers and leave the chocolates.
Are you afraid of tasting others' meanings,
lest you be overwhelmed by them?" This
last, with sadness and affection. Victoria,
shiny-eyed, says, "Welcome to you and
all your voices." Dante clears his throat
gruffly, and then leaves it at that.

Canto IX: Water On Parched Soil

Says the girl in the blue bikini, "Lucretia. My
name is Lucretia. Most folks call me
Lucy." Paul says, "Heaven is full of wonders, but
no surprises. Thank you for speaking,
daughter of pleasure and light. Thank you for opening
your circle to ours."
"That's all very nice, but what's this '*girl* in the
blue bikini' crap? I'm twenty-
nine! I'll bet, at least as old as that woman who
lives at number thirty. And, it's

turquoise, it's not blue!" Dante, gaze turned
somewhere up and to the right:
"As for that woman who lived at number thirty,
her years cannot be compared to
yours; life was different; she had fewer."
V says, "Please forgive our friend.
He intended no disrespect, I'm sure, by
using you to tease his teacher.
He is a visitor, new to here, and does not
fully comprehend the heavenly

law that one encounters no one, ever,
less than wholly and in the round.
I was remiss, not to remonstrate with him."
I say, "I apologize."
Lucy says, "You keep on talking like that,
it will not enhance your prospects,
reproductive-wise, not anywhere you'd
like to live. Oh, you could move to
where they dip their pickles in mayonnaise and
eat boiled peanuts. Eleven

years from now, the folks from there will give you
President I'm-So-Famous-I-Can-
Grab-A-Random-Woman-By-The-Pussy,
as he'll boast he does, and the women
there will mostly give him a pass on that, it's
just the kind of thing their guys say.
Jerks for men, the women are crushed and cynical –
sounds like a place you'll find a squeeze?"
"I will take my chances in the Northeast,
thanks. May I ask you, how you

overheard a conversation I thought
was occurring in my head? And,
how are you a prophet? The only prophets
I have heard from, up to now, were
not restricted – unlike us – to viewing
time through functioning physical organs."
"Ha ha! he has been admiring your organs,"
says Victoria. "Scuppered again," say
I; and Lucretia: "Nothing wrong with that.
I enjoy his admiration.

I was just relaying what our mutual
mentor, Mrs. Woodhull, whispered
in my pink and shell-like inner ear.
I'm a frequent flyer here.
I can tell when I am not alone."
"It's like sharing gossip with my
long-lost little sister," says Victoria.
Says Lucretia, "What you want to
know is, how is it I come here often?
Nobody living stays here long.

Sometimes it's as quick as a sneeze; sometimes
long as a slow, deep inhale;
sometimes, longer, if they want to keep you.
Bodies demand you concentrate, but
that is not what heaven is about.
We can't be aware of everything
all at once, all the time, the way they
do here; but sometimes, sort of.
Yoga helps, so does my work." I ask,
"What is that?" She answers, "Sacred

prostitute, twenty-first century California
style. Surrogate partner, we call it.
Help me explain it, Enkidu and Shamhat."
Muscled like a gymnast, a hairy,
short man with wild, green eyes and a
harsh voice: "Five thousand
years ago, it was written: A goddess
made me of mud and spittle, gifted
me with power, crafted me to befriend
Gilgamesh, the king, who had no

equal and so erupted in lonely supremacy,
swinging desire like an ax and breaking
men and women like clay dolls, finding
only hollow satisfactions.
I was naked and wild, in the woods. Animals'
wet noses touched me. I
ran alongside them, leaping over fallen
trees, and wrestled with them, besting my
friends the stags, and with the small ones I played
hide and seek. In the rain my

hair was as slick as their fur with water, it dripped from the
tips of my ears, nose and penis.
Where the traps and hunters lurked, I led my
friends away from. One day, roaming, I
came upon a pale and hairless image
of myself! It smelled of musk,
lying on the mold, upon its back,
limbs spread wide. It looked like
two paths made of moonlight crossing,
where they met a dark patch the

shape of a linden leaf, smelling of musk."
Soft, melodious, an alto
joins him. At the edges of her every
syllable, hints of laughter curl:
"Some of the trappers and hunters dared to lay their
grievances before Gilgamesh,
hoping not to be made corpses for calling on
his protection. But Gilgamesh was
wise in his wildness. Having taken counsel, he
sent to the temple where I lived, a

mother to my sisters, preserving women's
lore and wisdom, and serving men.
Gilgamesh charged me: find Enkidu, the wild man,
show him my body, and show him the things a
woman knows how to do; Gilgamesh,
trusting my power to be sufficient to
quell the wild man, the king's only equal.
So, I went to the forest. Anointed
with the appropriate oils, I lay where he was
sure to come upon me. He sniffed, then

mounted me, and covered me. What he
did, there are no words to describe,
just as animals have no words for fucking.
When he'd exhausted himself, he slept."
"Sudden, brutal, and quick, it shattered me.
Dawn came. I was alone.
All that day, I hunted her, until I was
fainting with weariness." "That was when I
chose to let him see me standing before him,
straight and tall." "This time, she and

I laid down together." "Thus his
education began. First, and
by the strongest measures, some quite painful,
I impressed upon him neither
he nor I might move upon the other
save with freely granted permission.
Then, my front to his back, my ear flattened
onto his warmth where it could follow
both his breath and his pulse, I waited, breathing
with him, feeling his heart slow its

moth-like flutter. When its pace matched mine, my
deep rhythm, and gave us space to
let me enter freely between the beats, I
touched him in a certain way."
"This was a thing I had not known, this helpless,
slowly quick, delicious spewing.
So we slept." "I hid again, next morning.
When I let him find me -" "I knew that
she'd find *me*!" "I taught him my name." "Shamhat."
Open-throated, the final vowel.

"I had allotted seven days for this work.
If, as some would have it, all the
world was made in this amount of time,
seven days should be sufficient for
me to bring a man to his humanity.
This third night, I taught him touch.
After we reclined together, my stomach
heating the dimples above his butt,
long enough for sweat to pool in them, I
peeled us apart and gave him a peach to

fondle with his curious fingertips.
Then we ate it, trading bites."
"Dribbling sweetness!" "Next, I had him bring his
hands to his feet, and legs, and arms, and
torso, neck, and face, and scalp, as he had
to the peach, and, as each part of him
spoke, I bade him tell me what it said."
"Dribbling sweetness!" "Then I let him
touch me as he'd touched himself, and I sang the
songs my body sang, for him.

When his fingers left my eyelids, brushing more
lightly over my eyebrows than he had
stepped, tracking deer, I began to
touch him, and he –" "Leaping and shuddering,
swift release overcame me." He sighs.
"I left him alone, next day;
but, before I left, I swiftly grazed his
half-awoken lips with mine."
"What was this new thing, I asked myself."
"That night, I showed him the art of

conversation with closed mouths."
"When I used this art to say I
wanted much to please her, then she showed me
how to speak in tongues." "Delirious
kisses, drunk on kissing. I grew wet, but
it was not yet time." "And, I was
shy of finishing early." "So, we slept. The
morning broke hot. I gave him a
farewell kiss. Shamash was kissing the treetops
when I returned to him, tomorrow's

lesson plan complete. I settled back on a
mound of moss and leaves that he had
gathered at my instruction, legs spread wide as the
wings of the palace Gilgamesh had
built in Uruk, facing Enkidu, and showed him
many-layered, hidden wonders,
slowly guiding his eyes as someday his eyes
slowly would be shown the inner
halls and rooms of Gilgamesh's palace.
Now, we exchanged places, and he

laid back and opened himself, and I served him
on a silver mirror the image
of those parts of him he'd never seen, the
puckered hole, the beautiful, chubby
lips that smiled in the same place my lips
smiled and held their secrets, and we
lingered also over that of his parts
most demanding of admiration.
Then I invited his eager hands on me,
face, arms, belly, legs and

breasts – " "Wonders!" "and sent mine to him.
Last, we touched those hidden places,
so alike in us, and so much different."
"Happily, I wet my belly, but
having more enjoyed what went before.
So we slept." "Again, the morning
broke hot. Today, the next to last, I
led him for miles and miles in sticky
heat to where my sisters had told me, 'bring him
here, that he may bear witness.'

Shamash was kissing the treetops when we reached the
small, square dwelling, where, her
body dominated by her belly,
squatted a woman giving birth."
"I had lived among animals. I had seen the
young come, pulsing and sliding,
out of their mothers, and the mothers lick them
clean and make them breathe and squall.
Why, then, did that world now seem so distant?
Why did I feel bitten free?

Why did my legs hold me shakily, leaning
on her, warmed and awed by her?"
"He was quiet as we went to rest in a
nearby meadow, quiet all day
sitting among the grasses and breeze-stroked flowers.
Lying there, that night, he rolled to
face me, and asked me, 'May I be the skin and
blood within your skin and blood?'
So I let him, for the second and the
last time, enter. And, we were done."

Paul says, "I was tinder for that sullen
conflagration that ate through millenia
like an unquenched coal seam fire, that
turned to ash in people's minds the
learning you speak of. Some of us burn in hell, for
lack of it." Lucretia answers,
"Riding in pure awareness; intending nothing
but my client's wholeness, and mine;
pouring this water on parched soil, and loving what
grows; often brings me here."

Canto X: More Schooling

Dante says, "I look directly over the
stirring waters and into the sun, and
on the horizon I see a dark speck, an
islet whose treetops the solar furnace
seems to be kissing, viewed from here and now.
Also, and at the present moment, that
same solar furnace fuels the winds
tearing the roofs off houses
in New Orleans, the rain, and the storm surge
drowning people in those houses.

In a few years, Inuit elders will see it
end the long winter night
early, rising from a strange direction
not known to living memory.
Warmer air atop snow-chilled air has
made a lens, and bent its light.
In my book, the sun was a figure for God.
On its movements, on the tilted
attitude of this earth to that single source of
all its light and heat, on the

consequent, unvarying, complex polyrhythms of
days and nights and seasons and years that
we had learned to play along with, like children
clumsily pounding on logs together
with a Master drummer, life depended.
Now, the children are driving the beat.
What you like to call your 'civilization'
prospers by incinerating
distillates of long-dead creatures, transmuting the
sunlight from which they built their bodies

into halitotic exhalations!
Midas and Icarus taught you nothing.
Lucy, Enkidu, and Shamhat were talking of teachers.
I met twelve in Paradise whose
knowledge, flowing from that lamp, sweetly
lighted my way. Have you known such?"
Says Enkidu, "She changed my way of thinking."
I say, "He's not talking to you.
He wants me to name my beloved instructors.
In first grade, Miss Vallet-Sandre.

Back then, schools hired artists to teach art,
as if art, as a matter of course, were
something every human should learn to do.
I remember one May morning, she
takes us outside to draw whatever we want that
can't be seen inside a classroom.
I am drawing the house across the street.
Sharp lines on brilliant paper.
She is leaning over my shoulder, and asking,
'Is that the lawn? Where is the grass?'

So, I broadcast clumps of little vees of
grass across the blankness. Now the
lawn is blankness pocked with little vees.
Now I fill it in, it's blank with
darkness. The house's outline hovers balloonishly.
When I hand it to her, she says,
lightly, like a joke that we both share, but
sharing too a tinge of sadness,
as if she knows that I know she knows,
'Oh! It's ruined' – teaching me the

joy and pain of making something I can
ruin, of striving to solve, as ever
since I've striven, such insoluble riddles:
Is that the lawn? Where is the grass?"
Dante: "Touching story, but purely personal.
Tell me, who revealed the world to
you, its setting, design, and workings; who mapped for
you the refractions through its borrowed
substance of the original maker and mover;
who named to you its angels and

demons; and not for you alone, but for all?"
"You know there is no such person!
Just about the time your ballistic arc through
Florence's finest began its ascent,
not long after to crash like a mortar shell,
William of Ockham forged in England a
blade so sharp and fine you cannot see it.
With it, we have slashed and flayed for
six or seven centuries the giant
carcass draped across our world of

your belief in a god who acts upon it,
peeling integuments, severing tendons,
hacking connective tissues. Sometime in the
past centennial, flensed from us, your
god succumbed to the death of a thousand cuts.
Many still thump the corpse's chest, like
tv medics who won't accept the tv
patient's heart is stopped, mistaking
their hysteric efforts for sustaining
rhythms; but, make no mistake about it,

god is coded. If our future science
were to winnow divinity from its
data, it would be an alien contact,
not rebirth or resuscitation."
As if talking to himself, D mutters,
"To what meeting are we taking you?"
I add, "Anarchy's loosed upon the world,
as a Poet said. But there are
many pretenders to the vacant throne.
When the Lord of Hosts and Ruler

of the Universe still was coughing up blood,
it was whispered in certain quarters that
Natural Science's chance of succession looked good. But,
in the end, extraction companies
staked their claim to geology, chemists were set to
fiddling with plastics and poisons for profit, the
lucrative diseases bought the attention of
medico-biological minds, and
physics, the highest and fairest of them all,
wound up lost as a kitten among a

snarl of superstrings, rolling on its
back and batting its paws at air,
mewing at darkness it can't see or explain but
thinks it suspects is probably there.
Human Reason, that House of warring houses,
had its champions. The Cult of Reason
lasted less than a year, in France, but flourished
nowhere else. Philosophers cluster in
little groups in urban centers, like exiles
after a revolution, mooting in

secretive idioms whether a meaningful statement
might be possible, and, if so,
what would such a statement look like? Not that
anyone cares, other than them."
"Like you modern American poets," says Dante.
I say, "Touché. And we, too, like to
think our revelations echo god's,
though we're mouthing only words,
not prodigiously gushing divine fanfares.
Energized by the All-Father's

death-spasms, mass movements spread,
bulked with the hearty fiber of their
leaders' thrilling oral and written instructions,
flushing out millions whose impulse to faith
proved tenacious when faith itself had faded.
Democrats, socialists, communists, fascists.
Two years after my birth, 'under god' was
added to the pledge we mumbled
every blessed day in the classroom, so we'd
know we were not godless Reds.

I liked saying 'freedom and justice for all.'
Faith may reside in aspiration,
as did mine, as lunging, snarling dogs,
water cannons, police batons, and
hooded incendiaries bloodied negroes for
asking politely to live like me.
I absolved myself of my other pledges, to
flag and nation, when Lyndon Johnson,
William Westmoreland, Robert MacNamara,
Dean Rusk, Henry Kissinger,

Richard Milhouse Nixon, McGeorge Bundy, and
Melvin Laird – you asked for my
teachers, not my mentors – insisted I honor
that condition imposed on all who,
in those days, sought recognition as a
man: you must be willing to kill on
orders from properly constituted authority.
Maybe their lies had something to do with it."
"In my day," says Dante, "demanding candor
from your prince was... well, you wouldn't.

So, as another teacher (yours?) might put it, the
arc of history over seven
centuries quivers almost imperceptibly
towards that mighty stream, justice.
Could one say, just like a *divin*ing rod?"
"Ha ha. Good one. And I'm grateful
that our oligarchs have found a means to
pass around power among themselves that
doesn't involve undue disturbance and murder, and
does allow me to run my mouth."

"Does it quiver towards justice?" "So I hope.
Here are the lessons I still have faith in.
Gödel taught me our most rigorous logic's
incomplete. Pema Chödrön
taught me comfort with uncertainty when
things, as always, fall apart. The
Dalai Lama taught me how compassion
binds us. Darwin... taught me. And, strangely,
Rabbi Steinsaltz taught me to see angels
in a thirteen petaled rose."

Canto XI: Franklin on Eleanor

While I'm talking, a very tall woman
pushes a wheelchair across the sand,
leaving no double furrow, approaching
us as I fall silent. The man in the
wheelchair says to her, "Babs, I told you so!
That's the fellow Abe saw at the
Presidential Library, that day I played
hooky from there," and, to me, with a
jaunty tilt of the head and a grin, "Hello!
What a pleasure it is to meet you!

What an interesting, important conversation
you are having. You are asking,
what is worthy of our devotion? May I
put my oar in? I know someone whose
life suggests an answer. Motherless and
fatherless before her teens, then
handed off to her grandma's frigid care, then
hi ho off to boarding school in
England, where they loved her, all the girls, and the
headmistress most of all. Father had

followed mother into the grave, but two years
after, of chronic overindulgence.
He was a sentimental drunk; although he was
somewhat neglectful during that time, she
idolized him, retrospectively, he
looked so well, next to grandma.
Not long after we first met, I called her an
angel. Perhaps indeed she was,
genuinely interested in every
human encounter, eager to learn and

help, always seeking our better selves.
Once we tied the knot, she revealed
further qualities I considered celestial –
six children in ten years! –
pouring all the energy she had left
after that into supporting
me in my endeavors and keeping the peace with her
husband's very active mother,
whose attachment to her only child
may have tried an angel's patience.

Measure our innocence by this: told by
someone babies need fresh air, she
hung our firstborn out the window in a
cage she'd made of chicken wire,
and I left her to it, until a neighbor,
much annoyed by the noise, complained.
When I announced my support for female suffrage,
she, heretofore shy of politics,
boldly followed my lead. Bolder still, she
disagreed with our formidable

family elders, calling it unfair that
rich men may avoid the draft by
hiring the poor to take their places. About this
time, while hiring household staff, she
met her first Negroes, as we called them,
whites being scarce due to the war.
Through their eyes, she first perceived race.
Some doors opened, some doors closed.
After she bore our sixth child, the medicos
ordered Babs to make no further

contributions of that kind to the world, a
disability that she greeted with
much relief; the burden of it pressed on
me much more than on her, abstinence
being the only certain way, those days, and
she did not much relish the act.
Popular opinion has it that this first,
callow phase of our lives ended
five years later, when I lost my legs to
'infantile paralysis.'

But, in fact, we hit the climacteric
months before my illness. I had
fallen for the woman I should have married,
had I sought light-hearted love and
not an earthly angel, adoration and
not a call to my higher nature.
How does that song go? 'You can't always
get what you want, but if you
try, sometimes, you get what you need.'
We exchanged letters. Eleanor found them.

She said later, 'The bottom dropped out of my
world. I faced myself, my surroundings, my
world, honestly for the first time.' A
disillusioned angel is no
less an angel. She is more of one.
We exchanged reciprocal offers of
freedom, which we reciprocally declined.
In a flash, she'd witnessed what we
were to one another, and what we were not.
My betrayal belonged to the realm of the

latter, which little mitigated her pain; our
bond held, but our distance grew, and
also – you may find this odd – our mutual
liking, affection, and respect.
She showed what fine stuff she was made of, nursing
pitiful me through months of crisis
so soon after our purgatorial season.
That done, her orbits widened
into the spheres of her own interests, becoming
her own person, always in service to

all the variously disadvantaged others
she embraced as each her own, and
bringing back to me her reports of the same.
So, she became my best informant
as to the lives of the people for whom I worked.
She even found - with a woman – what I had
found with Lucy, whom I had agreed
never to meet again, a promise I
broke, but only after twenty years.
My excuse for that transgression

is that, after two full terms, my final
weariness was setting in;
I knew chronic illness when I saw it;
war was eating away at the world; and
I could feel its claws, reaching for us.
I had accepted responsibilities
I could neither avoid nor easily master.
Sometimes, what makes us happy is also
what we need. I was sorely in need of the
strength that comes with joy, and took it."

Canto XII: Eleanor on Franklin

"I have little to add to what my husband
already told you of my childhood,
of my incapable mother, of my father
whom I adored but who was mostly
absent, and of my orphaned adolescence.
In my youth, I believed that nothing
in me would attract attention, much less
merit any admiration.
I was tall, unlovely, gawky, solemn,
timid, dreamy, not a dancer,

raised in social isolation by my parents,
and then by my grandma when they
passed me on to her; and she, judging
that her household was unsuitably
'too full of gaiety' for a girl of
fifteen, sent me overseas, for
finishing. There they treated me as someone
specially worthy to be properly
mothered. Several precious years of that, and
I was prepared to greet my cousin

Franklin's romantic attentions with gratitude and
not so much fear and confusion. He was
handsome, tall, athletic, charming, smart, with
values that, like mine, distanced
him from the self-important New York upper
crust to which we both were bred.
All he wanted to do was better those lower
down the social ladder than we were,
that is, just about everyone.
Knowing nothing of being in love,

I mistook my feelings – and his! – for that.
I agreed to marry him,
thinking my loneliness would find relief in his
largeness of heart. I was naïve,
but I was not altogether wrong,
though it proved more painful than I
could have dreamed. I had begun in a dream,
and I continued my dream of wifely
duty, loyalty, and sacrifice a
dozen years, dreaming myself as a

quiet conventional young society matron
upholding orthodox standards of goodness.
I awoke unpacking my husband's luggage,
holding his mistress's letters to him
in my shaking hand. Two years later,
when I was nursing his convalescence,
running the household, mothering five children,
fending off my mother-in-law's
constant interventions, keeping in touch with the
vast number of contacts we needed to

keep his career alive, and doggedly following
my own path that had opened before me
since that dreadful instant of clarity, a
day came when I broke into sobs that
would not stop. The bargain I had struck to
stay his wife looked bleak, then.
That was my one time of going to pieces.
I had been so wrong about what
Franklin needed me for, and what I could give him.
He, who misjudged rarely if ever,

had, by contrast, nothing to revise in
what he knew or asked of me. His
grief for the loss of his love left me untouched,
save by the deeper kindness it bred in him.
He treated me ever only with kindness,
unlike those who blame or hate the
person they have wronged, and trusted me in
matters important to him, although
intimacy, as such, was over between us,
just as if it never had been.

You may think that I digress to the merely
personal; where else would one find the
roots of greatness? I could name his accomplishments,
but to you young people it would
be a boring recital of long forgotten
programs and things you take for granted.
He had such a gift for life! He gave us
strength and security. The polio year, he
took it on himself to cheer up all of
us, his caregivers, as if the cruel,

unrelenting illness afflicted us, not
him, reserving his depression
for the mornings, when he stayed in bed and
did not have to be gotten up.
Our generation was taught from childhood to wear a
stiff upper lip over suffering.
Many thought that meant to bite it back.
Franklin managed his troubles by helping
us to bear the burdens they imposed.
Here was a difference between him and me:

he would not have understood my motto,
*You must do the thing you think you
cannot do*, because the last five words were
quite beyond him. *You must do the
thing that needs to be done*, he would have said.
He fought through the initial crisis,
when at times his weakness would not let him
hold a pen, until we allowed him
visitors. They revived him. He lived for people.
Locking his legs in fourteen pounds of

steel, he practiced a form of ambulation.
Hips too weak to support him, he would
pivot from crutch to crutch by swinging his head and
torso from side to side, two hundred
feet to the driveway's bottom, pouring sweat.
Having agreed to remain his wife,
I did what was needed, tending to his
humbler needs and keeping political
contacts active. Forty years of age, he
had it all ahead of him. His

mother argued for him to retire to a
quiet country life – imagine!
Fortunately, we persuaded him to
follow his own inclination.
I must tell you about his wheelchair. It was
central to the events that showed me
he was more than my companion through whom
so many doors were opened to me,
more than chief among the many we knew
who had accomplished worthwhile things, but

someone great." "An accolade from an angel!"
he says. She says, "He designed it,
cobbled together a kitchen chair, some wheels, and of
course an ashtray on the arm.
That was his conveyance the rest of his life.
Sitting in it, he spoke to Congress a
month before his passing, and asked their pardon for
not addressing them from his feet,
as he had on every previous occasion.
Never before had he been wheeled

down the aisle among them, or acknowledged
that his legs were useless, in public.
Until then, it was akin to a point of
faith among us that American
voters couldn't accept a crippled leader:
never, never let the public
view the wheelchair. That was our deception."
"I was proud of my little ashtray."
"Hush, you. Only twice did Franklin allow
strangers in public places to see his

true condition. First, in thirty-six, at
Howard University. He was
there to dedicate their newest building.
He was photographed, as usual,
screened by the podium, propped up on his feet.
What no picture shows is how he
got there. Howard's president had asked my
husband to offer the students, crippled
as their prospects were by white hostility,
inspiration. Before their eyes,

Franklin had himself lifted from his car,
lowered to the pavement, locked in his
braces, and man-handled to the stage." Franklin
interjects, "It was a carefully
calculated act of self-exposure,
like a stripper wearing a wetsuit.
Just a week to go, before my expected
sweeping, landslide victory
for a second and I thought final term; and
what were the odds that any voter

likely to desert me over such hijinks was
likely to notice whatever might happen at
Howard." Eleanor continues, "The
second event was in forty-four,
while you were touring Pacific military
installations. In Honolulu,
you took advantage of a hiatus in meetings
with the 'brass' to quietly visit
soldiers and sailors in amputation wards,
asking your Secret Service guard to

wheel you through. You took your time. You stopped at
one bed after another,
talked with the unfortunate young people
from whom limbs had been removed,
gave them time to see and take you in,
while you exchanged your small talk.
That was when you were greater than your office, in
my opinion." Franklin says, "Dearest,
"those respects I so cheaply paid, bought me
leave from the Presidential Library."

Canto XIII: The Marriage Of Heaven And Earth

    Franklin leaps from his wheelchair and wingfoots a jig to
        Eleanor's stylings on the harmonica.
    Smiling, Lucretia takes Dante's hand, Victoria
    mine, and we join them. I send sand-clouds
    glittering ankle high in the morning light.
        Paul prances partnerless, then
    grabs Enkidu's waving fist and leads him
    past Shamhat. Enkidu embraces her
    waist, and we're a foam-footed conga line,
kicking and leaping to welcome the waves, the

    blazing sun-shard highway they bear to us.
    "Where did you learn to blow harp?" I
    ask Eleanor, after Franklin's resumed his
    seat and I've recovered my breath.
    But, before she answers, Victoria cuts in:
        "Had your customary sharpness
    not been blown to breathless flinders by her
        instrumental virtuosity,
what did you intend to ask these lovebirds?"
    "What brought you together?" I ask.

E. says, "People marry without the faintest
notion what they're taking on, and
I the least of all.   He was tall,
handsome, athletic, the whole world
knows how charming, going places, wanting to
better people's lives, attentive to
what I said and thought – appreciative, yes! of my
mind, as if *of course* I had one:
that was terrifyingly irresistible."
F: "From early youth, I knew that

my preferred career would lead me into
close collaboration with devils.
So I needed an angel by my side, to
keep me balanced on my feet.
I don't say I knew I had that need or
set out consciously to fill it...."
"I was one of those who served his purposes,
as a wife was supposed to do.
After the light broke upon me, I served his
purposes better by serving my own."

Dante offers, "Even though you did not
know your reasons, or, knowing some, you
did not know them all, and even though the
ones you thought you knew you did not
understand, and even though you knew you
did not know what you were doing,
nevertheless, you bravely faced what called you,
as a sleeper, abruptly awoken, may
choose, instead of hiding in bed, to grope for the
wakener; for that moment, only that

motion is real." I say, "Victoria, see how
gently Dante nudges me forward,
in the direction he wants me to go; but you, by
contrast, elbow me in the ribs.
So," I say to Franklin and Eleanor, "muddled
as your motives for marrying were,
Franklin's affair with Lucy was a betrayal, but
not a mistake?" E says, "I was
stunned by pain and silly with propriety.
Had he been honest with me, had he been

capable of that sort of honesty, I would
not have understood him." Franklin:
"My mistakes began when we lost Louis; and
gosh, I made some whoppers, then!"
E: "That dear, odd little man! I thought him
sour, at first, and was put off by
that and by the odor of burnt tobacco that
always clung around him, but then,
during our ordeal of Franklin's illness, he
took me beneath his wing and showed me

what devotion meant and how to use my
talents, that I hardly knew of,
in our common service to my husband; and
if a sharp and capacious intellect,
focused by keen vision through a large and
loving heart upon our world,
seems to produce tartness, then, so be it."
I say, "What mistakes? Such as?"
"Let us now praise Louis Howe, who held my
feet quite firmly to the ground, and

kept them pointed in the direction both of us
wanted them to go, and mastered the
art of saying 'no' so I could hear it,"
Franklin says. "What about the
Japanese internment?" I ask. Franklin:
"Louis was long gone, by the time I
signed that Order granting the Army license to
do the thing I knew they would,
in the name of wartime coastal security.
Dead persons do not indulge in

counterfactuals, so I cannot ask him
what advice he would have given.
He was that wise navigator who read the
stars and weather signs, knew the
shoals and rocks and channels in every harbor,
checked my bearings, kept me on course.
He'd have been no use to me if I had
known in advance what he would say."
Eleanor: "Nonsense, my dear, you know as well as
I that he'd have opposed it with all the

vigor he could muster – as I tried to
tell you, but you said you did not
wish to talk with me about that subject."
Franklin: "Louis had within him
just enough of the devil so that he could
speak to all of me, heart and mind.
These are the kinds of things that happened after he
left me, alone in the Rose Garden.
You exhorted me to do the right thing,
throw the weight of my support to

legislation that might discourage local
law enforcement from ignoring
racial atrocities, such as then were all too
regular in our southern states.
That was 1937, the year that,
nearly having scaled the walls of the
sinkhole that had opened under us on
Black Friday, we slipped at the lip.
Who knew how far we might slide back down?"
Eleanor: "In my travels, I met

families living in dirt-floored animal coops,
bunking two to a bed for warmth, and
groups of children brought to greet me (so their
keepers told me) 'from the mill',
whom I labored to describe for the readers
of my positive-minded, cheerful,
forward-looking, daily newspaper column.
It is hard to be honest without
also being candid. These 'delicate' children,
I wrote, needed 'a good big bowl of

bread and milk' more than my whistle-stop visit, for
which they appeared to be unenthused."
"Yes," says Franklin, "that was the setting. I said,
'I did not choose the tools with which I
must work. Had I been permitted to
choose them I would have selected
quite different ones. But I've got to
get legislation passed to
save America. Southerners, by reason of the
Congress' seniority rules, are chairmen or

occupy strategic places in most of the
Senate and House committees. If I
come out for the anti-lynching bill now,
they will block every bill I
ask Congress to pass. I just can't risk that.'
That was me, telling myself I
knew what Louis would have advised me to do,
one year after we were bereft of him.
Do I contradict myself? On one hand,
how could I know what he'd say? And,

on the other, I flogged my brain to tell me
that very unknowable thing!
Missing him, I called to mind our talks and
our political calculus - meaning the
word in both its senses, a method of reasoning
and an accretion of hardness. It was
like a conditioned reflex, such as we who've
been in power long enough to
be infected by it may develop.
Like a conditioned reflex, what it

lacked was reference to a living reality
outside my own mind, such as
Louis so adeptly used to help me
find my place in relation to."
"What you say suggests an explanation
for the Japanese internment
and the 'repatriation' of Mexicans, so-called,
but you do not offer excuses,"
E says. Dante chimes in, "Hear, hear."
F says, "Absolutely right."

"When we sacrifice what seems to us the
lesser interest to the greater,
not unless what seems to us the lesser
interest is in fact our own
does there anywhere exist a scale on
which to measure, without bias,
one world's substance against another's,"
Eleanor says. "*Davvero*," says Dante,
"yet, in office, to do just that, people
and events call us unceasingly."

Canto XIV: We Are Dawash Of Akhvilli!

Somebody's strumming an umpapa waltz on a roughly-tuned
cheapo guitar, Enkidu, singing
Woody Guthrie's elegiac ballad for
migrant Mexican farm workers killed when the
airplane they were riding homewards crashed at
Los Gatos Canyon: "Good-bye to my
Juan, good-bye Rosalita... adios mes amigos
Jesus y Maria... you won't have a name when you
ride the big airplane... all they will call you will be
deportees." Afterwards, silence.

All of a sudden, then, the sand in the center
of our circle puckers; rises, a
tan-gold pimple; mounds; extends, columnar,
reaching the height of a person; extrudes
two tubular limbs at what might be shoulders;
splits below, leg-like; pinches
tight, a neck; pimpling forth on the spud-like
head, a nose, and furrowing there in
bas-relief a mouth and eyes; unfurling
just like spring's first leaves, two ears.

"I am Dawash of Akhvilli," it says,
sprouting a penis. Beside him, another
bursts upward; its breasts balloon; labial
creases appear between its legs as
if an invisible finger draws in the sand.
"We are Akhvilli Dawash," it says.
Sandy-voiced, they speak together: "Welcome,
fleshly travelers, to this stratum!"
Says Lucretia, "Wow! I'm dreaming, right?"
Choruses Dawash, "Almost always!

At this place and moment, not so much!"
I say, "Dreaming has words, but no language.
Dreams, like North Korean abductors, whisk us
all the way across the border, for
reasons obscure, to strange fermentations
we can barely describe to ourselves.
You and I both came here voluntarily.
I came at this gentleman's beck, in
hopes of finding my way to love; and though I'd
swear I am not dreaming, weirdness has

met my every step like rose petals
scattered on the sidewalk before me."
"Hey," says Lucretia, "Where's Enkidu? Shamhat?
Paul and Franklin?" Eleanor answers,
"They are where, for the most part, they belong."
"This is getting too trippy for me,"
Lucy says, extending her arms to me.
Air hug? Farewell wave?
In my eyes, standing before me, she fades,
fleetingly translucent, a sun-rouged

wisp of cloud behind her showing through.
Then she's lying on her blanket,
solid as the trees she's lying under.
I say, "Eleanor, you're still with me?"
She says, "As my husband might have put it,
chairing eighty-three diplomatic
meetings, as I did to bring into being the
Universal Declaration of
Human Rights, came mighty close to martyrdom.
Maybe that's why I'm still here!

As this beach transforms itself from level to
level of heaven, while staying the same,
so the nations I cajoled to grant their
peoples the right to decent treatment by
those who, consented or not, presume to govern,
rose a notch by so agreeing."
Just now, sand erupts again, around us.
"Dawash of Akhvilli welcome!" they
grittily trumpet, a joyous tandem fanfare.
In the storm's clear eye, we

huddle, the women, Dante, and me, surrounded by
whirling columns of flagpole height.
"Dust devils," I whisper. V. replies,
"Dust angels. Look, it slackens."
Slowing, they shorten and densify. Another
blast of "Dawash Akhvilli welcome!"
Faces condense and carousel around us.
"I am Anwar. For daring to touch my
palm to my brother Menachem's, I was slain."
Each, passing, announces itself:

"I am Johnny Maguire, deceased in my second
year of life, one day after
Danny Lennon lost control of his car from
shooting and them shooting back, and
ran me over and my brother and sister,
so Aunt Mairead was inspired to
join the thousands of Irish women becoming
those who will inherit the earth."
"I am Richard Holbrooke." ("But he's alive," I
whisper. "So are you," says V.)

"I am Jigonsahseh, Mother of Nations.
In my lodge, no passing warrior
was unsafe, unfed, or uncared for.
By my hearth, the man whose name means
Two River Currents Flowing Together
found a new mind; from our
joined brows Hodenosaunee was born."
"I am Maximilian, son of
Fabius Victor, beheaded by Cassius Dio
for refusing to bear arms.

His empire is history; mine's in the making."
(Dante salutes him on bended knee.)
"Jeannette Rankin here, Montana's gift to
gender equality, first female
member of the U.S. Congress, where I
joined the forty-nine who voted
not to enter Mr. Wilson's so-called
'war to end all wars' because the
first woman who had a chance to say no to
war, should say it. Just like Crystal

Gawding, Comfort Freeman, Leymah Gbowee,
Ellen Johnson Sirleaf, and hundreds of
fed-up women said to Charles Taylor, and
Barbara Lee told Dubya Bush."
(V. says, "Women," and elbows me in the ribs.
"Yes," I say, "I get it.") BOOM!
Sand spouts anew around us, towering
tan columns, scores of them! The
six who've spoken revolve around us clockwise;
counterclockwise, the next ring;

outside it, another dances deasil; the
last one orbits widdershins.
Eleanor laughs and claps her hands: "Oh!
I so hoped that he would come!"
Visages surface from within the fountaining
columns, stacked from crown to chin to
crown to chin in sabulous totem poles,
arcs converging overhead to
criss-cross on a shield-shaped cloud,
like a gothic ceiling's tracery

or a mandala constantly weaving itself.
In the shield, an intelligent face, a
kind and wary face, with questioning eyes, a
broad, long, straight nose,
wide lips that may smile, sometimes, a
short chin covered by a
white soul patch that merges into
a petite and neat goatee,
sturdily built, rectangularly framed by
frizzy curls in an upside-down "U."

"Trauttmannsdorff! Two ens, two effs, three tees!
At your service, my friends!" he says.
V. leaps in: "Your Excellency, we have
here a pilgrim, a noncombatant.
All his youth, his nation fought to stabilize
dominoes it kept knocking over,
and to avenge an attack that never occurred.
Now, it fights to save the world from
nonexistent weapons. Hopeless, meaningless;
only the deaths are real. He despairs."

Eleanor: "It might help if you could tell him
what you did to win your place here."
"Oh, I did not come to hear hosannas
sung in my poor name. The Emperor
I served wanted peace and gave me what I
needed to serve as midwife to it.
Five years' talking ended thirty years' brawling,
pillaging, raping, starving, untimely
dying weapon-pierced or rotted by illness.
He had other motives, of course; we

termed them more exalted, Reasons of State;
he was, like his peasants, afraid that
They will snatch the grass from his children's lips,
burn his house down over their heads.
Likewise, also, these two hundred and thirty-five
excellencies parading around in
all their charming complexity, my former
colleagues and interlocutors, who –
meaning to cast no shade on your achievement,
Mrs. R., nor to belittle your

fourscore meetings – met in bilateral groups,
with no chair, and never gathered in
plenary session. *Ach! Mein Gott!*
If, in international fora,
you are represented as belonging to
something that can be drawn on a map, and
not as subject to someone's personal interests,
that was one of our innovations;
also, international fora, as such.
In the spirit of our genial

hosts, *willkommen in meiner Welt, mein Freund."*
"Since you mention the Dawash," I say,
"please, tell me what they are doing here?" But,
faster than you can say "Akhvilli," the
beach breeze swells, eroding our sandy
company into a formless cloud soon
disappearing in the distance, leaving us
lightly dusted. Dante says,
"I should think it would be obvious to you.
They are here for welcoming strangers."

Canto XV: Building The Workers' Paradise

Squatting over a tide pool, I splash my face,
rinsing grains to glitter bottomwards.
"You were curled up much that way when first I
found you in the wastelands," says Dante.
"Foetal, but on his feet," Victoria says.
"Say what feelings you brought to that meeting," the
Master Poet adjures me. I say, "I was
desolated, at that time, by a
fickle lover's betrayal, or so I called it;
and the country I thought I'd known,

like the lover I thought I'd known, turning
out to be something unimagined,
distant, alien. I know now I chose as
lovers those who would not go the
distance, hedging against greater loss; the
ineluctable, greatest loss some
day would come around the corner and find me
crouched there, as it were, already
cutting my life short. To say it is to
know it can be otherwise,

heart rapping the bars of its cage and my breath
pumping sharp and fast and clear.
How I wish I'd feel a similar quickening,
contemplating my compatriots!
Fearful, distractible, ignorant dupes, addicted to
endless addictions – they make me tired."
Glittery grains, resisting gravity, swirling
longer than they should, collect in the
tide pool, forming a tiny, golden saurian.
It climbs onto the back of my hand with

little, prickling claws, and, lifted to eye level,
it says, "This is your problem. You want to
know what is your problem? I will tell you."
Midway between a croak and a purr, the
voice is familiar, but I can't quite place it.
Pouring velvet coated gravel,
it continues, "What do you think you want from
talking monkeys doing what talking
monkeys do, protecting their troop and caring
for their children? You expect more?"

Then it hits me. I say, "You were up to the
eyeballs, poaching in Anger like a
matzoh ball in chicken soup, when I
saw you last. Now you're Here!
How did you pass over?" He says, "Ha ha!
Yes, I ferried you and Mister
What-A-Friend-We-Have-In-Jesus on my
back across the boiling river."
Dante bends a knee. The croc says, "Welcome.
Also, I enjoyed our talk.

So... you wonder how you could have found me
there below and here, as well.
There, one only sees the shit he sank in.
Here, is a beautiful, sunny beach.
How am I both places? I was three men."
I say, "Zaide, visiting in your
house when I was little, I remember
this strange atmosphere, as if
normal, everyday feeling, happiness even, was
disconnected from the ground, like

when you flick a water droplet onto a
hot griddle, and it dances."
"That," he says, "was the anger beneath.
Also, another me lived there, you
didn't get to meet him much; he didn't
like to peek his head up where it
might get cut off. It wasn't a happy marriage.
Him, you learned about from the telling.
I complained you kids knew nothing of my
struggles, but who was I talking about? The

one who kvetched was not the one who engaged in
struggle. Let me tell you a story: my
first meal in the New World. The shtetl I
came from, in Ukraine, you wouldn't
know the name. When I left, it was managing –
barely! – to survive its neighbors'
Christian hostility and indifference, like a
man hugging himself to keep
warm in winter, seven hundred years.
No books but religious books.

No news but by word of mouth when someone
came back home from visiting relatives.
No political parties, actions, issues.
Not enough to eat, and nothing
much to do. A permanent refugee camp.
I outlived it. You've got cousins who
weren't so lucky. When I was seven, my father, a
shoemaker, left for the land of freedom and
maybe a happier life, and I became the
man of the house. Nine years later, he

sent for me a ticket. So... I left the
cabbage, potatoes, onions, beets, a
piece of chicken or beef on special occasions.
I was sixteen, not a sailor,
very skinny by the time we finally
entered the harbor, saw the Statue,
passed through Ellis Island, docked at the pier,
stepped onto pavement so excited I
almost wasn't aware how hungry I was.
Nothing prepares you for New York.

Through the gaps among the passing people,
I could see across the street a
cart heaped with red and green fruit. I
said to myself, 'ikh vel onheybn meyn
nay lebn durkh esn an epl,' having no
English — I'll start my new life with an
apple. My first bite, I spit it out!
'Oy! Dem epl iz farfoylt,' I
stopped myself from saying. Rotten apples, I
knew from home. This was different.

So, fresh off the dock, my first tomato.
It was a stormy and interesting life.
After a year, my father, who sent for me to
come to him in the New World and
found me a job in the needle trades, kicked me
out of his home because he could not
live with someone who didn't believe in god.
'Ven iz meyn nomen gevarn Itzkhok', I
said on the way out the door, but he didn't get it.
I had learned to disbelieve in god from the

socialists, anarchists, syndicalists, progressives,
communists – Leninists, Stalinists, Trotskyists,
Lovestonites – agitating and organizing
in the workplace and on the streets to
which my father called me. Them, and the thousands
working sixty hours a week for
miserable wages in sweatshop conditions, happy to
have a job they might lose any
day for any reason, with nothing to help them
if they were unemployed or sick.

These I called my brothers and sisters. A hundred
years before your Mr. Bush
hit his trifecta, I saw bodies falling
down the sides of a tall building,
less frightened of hitting the pavement than of
burning behind the factory doors the
bosses had locked to keep them at their machines.
That was when I joined the union.
Over years of fighting so my brothers and
sisters should have lives of comfort,

happiness, dignity, and respect, I rise to
full time union office. I'm
transferred West, to lead a painful, secret,
also bloody struggle against the
comrades who still believed in the soviet promise.
After, it's like occupying and
reconstructing a city ruined by warfare.
And, for me, New York was not the
real melting pot; that was Los Angeles,
where I'm almost alone with my Yiddish

and the needle workers I'm representing are
mostly black and Mexican women.
When I demanded the union treat them fairly,
I found brothers and sisters I never
knew I had. That is when I sank my
claws into these sands. Sure, the
storms continued. Tell me what family they don't? But
I, a Jew not a stranger, knew to
whom I belonged. Look - you see the horizon?
That's not nearly where it ends."

Canto XVI: Sacrament Of My Grandfather

"Holy Moses! I mean Bob, the guru of
SNCC and the Freedom Summer, and also the
guy who led us out of Egypt. Wow!
It was the fifties! You, my zaide,
marching side by side with my childhood heroes!
Martin Luther King! Rosa
Parks! Bayard Rustin! Fanny Lou Hamer!"
Rhapsodizing thus, I turn to
V. and catch her hiding a smile. I ask her,
"What's so funny?" She says, "You,

marching in the footsteps of the footsteps."
Dante cackles, "Just as someone
stumbles step by step along a path through
freshly fallen, heavy snow."
"So my grandpa's virtues puff me up!
Here is someone worthy of reverence!
During his life, I kept my distance from him;
and his struggles, and their fruits,
sounded to me like echoes rising from deep in a
well of anger." "That is the hell of it,"

he says. I say, "I am sad I stayed at
arm's length until death's
stony rim walled you safely off; and
leaning over, I now look in.
There's your heritage, at the bottom, gleaming!
What frustration, that your living
eyes never saw it shining in mine! The
gifts came late; but here is love."
Gently, Victoria's arm twines with mine.
I'm so thrilled, I almost fail to

hear her whisper, "We'll not tease you, now you
show us joy." If I could, I'd
turn the whole of my attention to her;
but, my zaide's unmuffled basso
grinds into gear and could not be denied
even if the will to deny it
had not left me, leaving only
tender rawness. "Never too late!
Would it have been gratifying? Yes; but
heartwarming moments don't mean much.

Listen: my new brothers and sisters cost me
friends I'd had for decades, and in the
bitter end, they wanted one of their own to
sit at the head of the table, not a
New York Jewish alte kaker. Feh!
Life is bitter. Being a Jew,
I could guess at most of what they'd suffered.
That was not enough for them.
Why should anyone care for someone else's
sorrow? The comfort of crying together?

Who would want such second-hand compassion?"
"Women have discovered the greatest
strength in sharing stories," says Victoria.
I say, "Yes, and some men, too."
"This was not my motivation. I did
not seek warm and cozy feelings.
In my heart, all I wanted to know was,
was I fair to my brothers and sisters,
did I work for all of them the same for
social justice, human dignity,

economic opportunity?" I say,
"That could seem cold." He replies,
"Who is a friend? Someone who dries your tears, or
someone who wouldn't make you cry?
When I say for me the most important
thing was, am I fair, I don't mean
what you learned about fairness in school. They taught you
what the bosses want workers to think."
I can feel him watch with me the *red
rubber ball as it streaks* in memory

*over the playground's mangy grass. Having
kicked it past the infield, Bobbie
runs to second. "She didn't touch first!" yells Sam.
"Yes I did!" "Oh no you didn't!"
Contradictions threaten to fly into fisticuffs.
Arms wave. Shrill shouts.
Charlotte snivels. The teacher raises her voice.
Faces swivel. Into expectant
silence, she hands down her adjudication.*
He continues, "It's a benefit

they might give if they decide they want to,
if they think it's worth it to them."
*Hundreds of arms lifted and waving fists in
rhythmic unison with deeply
angry voices punch the air, demanding
peace.* As Zaide listens, *a cop who's
old enough to be my father tells me,
kindly, "It's the younger ones who
like to bust your heads." Crash of shattering
glass behind us draws our suddenly*

concentrated attention. Grandpa goes on,
"So you yell at the grownups you want
they should end the war, stop pollution,
vote for this or that, free
all political prisoners, feed the poor,
make society fair and just.
Disappointment after disappointment.
Some become discouraged, and quit.
Life is hard enough, for them, without they
try to make it better. Many

so-called revolutionaries lose their
faith in grownups, turn instead to
sex and drugs and comforting kinds of religion, or
try with loudness, rudeness, violence
so the grownups pay attention, but the
grownups only say don't be so
loud and rude and violent, and the sacred
cause becomes a circus sideshow.
Just a few struggle on. These are
mostly beaten, jailed, ignored.

Sometimes they win, and then they're labeled heroes
so you'll think they're not like you."
I say, "Yes, you're right, that's how it is."
He says, "We hungry outsiders
learned a different sort of lessons about
fairness in our new-found home.
I'm not talking Jewish immigrants only.
Also blacks and Mexicans, fleeing
by the millions poverty, lynchings, laws the
Nazis used as models – I would

never have to waste much breath explaining
what's a pogrom, to a black.
We learned young your country is the same like
any, ruled by wealth and privilege.
You're a greenhorn seeking a better life?
They don't want a person seeking
any kind of better; too much trouble,
by them everything's okay.
They want someone who will work for cheap,
ask for nothing, live invisibly,

quit when body and mind are all worn out,
go home quietly, and die.
You don't ask for fairness. They don't give you
fairness, not unless they have to.
Fairness, you take, from people who call you goniff,
thief, for making them let you have it,
bit by bit. A bissel is what you get,
never all at once: a minimum
wage; a week of forty hours in a
place that shouldn't kill or sicken;

something you can live on when you're older."
"Each a gem," says Dante, "grabbed at
risk from the dragons' hoard. They plot forever
how to force you to give it back."
"Fairness, I learned to carry in my gut, a
stone the strongest punches could not
break, fuel that's never exhausted, compass that
always gave me true direction.
Some of that rage, my boychik, I passed to you," he
says. "Sacred rage," says Dante.

Canto XVII: A History Lesson

I say, "Were you happy to see your bequest
turned against the government?"
He says, "You, meyn ainikle, brought me nakhes.
If I had seen less of me in
you, still I would have said, dayenu.
But, do you want I should have been
sad, that you're a fighter?" Now he shows to
me the sweet and fleeting smile that
I recall redeemed some childhood moments.
I smile back. I say, "I know

every thought of mine is open to you."
V. says, "What you like to think are
'your' thoughts can't be fully known to you,
if you don't articulate them."
"Ask away," says Zaide. I say, "Okay.
Once upon a time you were as
wealthy as me: you owned a body." He says,
"No, I rented." "And, you clung to
your opinions, wouldn't give them up, not
even to keep a roof overhead, or

maybe you rode them like a raft out of your
father's home, I wouldn't know.
Now, you've left the realm of mere beliefs and
multi-purpose mental tools.
In your disagreement with your father,
who was closest to the truth?"
He says, "Meyn foter and I reconciled.
So, we both were equally close.
More I cannot say in any way that
would be meaningful to you.

You will find out for yourself, maybe
while your skull and skin still hold you,
maybe when they open and let you out.
On this beach, you'll maybe catch a
glimpse of what I'm talking about." Silence.
Eyes as calm and yellow and unrevealing as
if he's lying on a mudflat, watching
me float by. It's up to me:
"Then, perhaps, you might expand, Mister
Sub Specie Aeternitatis,

on the subject of rich elites. When the
people care, the people win –
is that not America's gift to the world?"
He says, "Hoo ha! You will get a
longer answer maybe than you wanted.
First, you have to understand:
Nothing was easy. For everything, we fought.
You, who never had to fight for
any good your country gave you, may not
understand the gratitude and

love I felt at having been allowed to
force it to give me a better life,
even grudging and at the cost of blood,
more precious because of that.
Nu, farshtayst?" I say, "Yes, I think so.
And to hear you rank me privileged,
therefore not entirely deserving, well, it
hurts; but yes, it's true enough.
Still, it's also fair to remind you, I came of
age in the draft, and wanting neither to

kill or be killed, maybe never and certainly
not in the service of lies, stupidities,
and corrupt oppressions, I had to make some
choices that weren't choices." He says,
"So, you went to college." I say, "It was
that, or prison, or Canada. I was
favored in many ways. I wasn't free.
After the last helicopters
lurched away from the embassy's roof, with their
desperate cargoes, this sourness lasted.

Like the sea that swallowed those choppers when they
finished that mission, public opinion
finally closed over the heads of the hawks.
Doesn't that make my case? If so,
I remember I took no pleasure in winning."
He says, "Good, then it won't spoil your
happiness when I say Nixon, not the
people, brought the troops home, when he
found the war no longer served his purposes.
Listen: a hundred years already,

long before your so-called gift-to-the-world was
given to people who didn't know yet
what to do with it, two contending
forms of organization appeared in the
world, to shape, control, and profit from it.
First, business corporations. The
Brits and then the Dutch invented them to
squeeze better their overseas colonies.
Not long after, my friend Trauttmannsdorff –
you have met him? – and his colleagues

cooked up what you're living in today.
Time was, where you lived was a bundle of
loyalties, interests, and family relationships
tied to a ruler. Now, you live in a
piece of land with people on it and borders
only a gonif state, a paskudnyak, would
violate, invade, or enter to meddle."
Dante can't help cutting in:
"Like twin gods, these newborns grew to
straddle the earth while the old gods,

helpless against them, slowly faded away.
Sometimes colluding, rarely conflicting, at
least not openly, the youthful deities
jointly established their mutual sway.
Always, the brawny, younger sibling bawled of its
primacy, while the wily elder
gathered strength and the means to fend away or
buy off junior's crude coercions.
Always, they stand shoulder to shoulder with fingers
at each other's throats, professing the

greatest affection for the common herd."
"Thank you for the interruption,"
Zaide says, "but you left out how junior
got the jump on the older sibling.
Junior improved and built on something already
that existed. The older sibling
had to build from scratch, under governments'
watchful eyes. Three hundred years, it
took the older sibling to catch up,
in the time and place I tasted my

first tomato, in the New World."
Dante: "So, the gods dance,
oligarchs strewing flowers at their feet and
cashing in on their many blessings.
But, there is a third, the youngest, barely
out of infancy, busily dodging the
stomping steps, almost overlooked."
Zaide: "When the merchants, bankers,
owners of real estate and slaves, investors,
planters, lawyers, and gentlemen of

means in America figured out they'd get a
better deal by paying taxes
to themselves instead of bending the loyal
knee to their colonial master,
Jefferson named the price they'd pay for quiet
marketplaces, streets, and workshops
so they could pass power back and forth
undisturbed among themselves:
say 'all men are created equal' and act as
if, but only when you must."

V. says, "Not all wealthy persons lack all
decency, humane compassion, and
honor. Not entirely." Z. says, "Maybe
so, but when you sift their ashes,
you will not find any pearls." I say,
"That's so bleak!" "Don't forget the
baby," he says, "One thing they're afraid of:
workers uniting for each other.
If you want democracy, join a union.
Solidarity forever!"

Canto XVIII: Guilty Of Enticing Others Likewise

On the strand just north of us, a mixed
flock of sandpipers, mostly godwits,
suddenly leaves its stiff-legged skittering; launches
skyward, a graceful, amorphous blob;
stretches, condenses, extends a pseudopod that
veers and refolds into the main; and
shifting, flowing, the mass of backlit bodies
halts in front of the sun! Dark
specks pointillistically portray a
heavy-jawed human face. The

jaw moves up and down! The thick, broad
lips work as if forming the words that
seem to issue from the birds' peeping
and the hissing of the waves.
"Isaac Robinson of Massachusetts.
Right about the time those Dutchmen
and those German diplomats were laying
your world's foundation stones,
I got sentenced to dozens of whippings for running and
also enticing others likewise."

Now the flock flies through a series of portraits,
reconfiguring so fast it
blurs into a single, haunting image, a
hollow-eyed, pinch-cheeked
child. She speaks: "We served the machines
weaving cloth in the Paterson mills
sixty-nine hours a week. In 'twenty-eight we
walked out 'cause our lunch was
moved from noon to one and we were afeared they'd
take it away. They called the militia to

break us, but we got our lunch hour back." The
slide show snaps to a stop on a soft,
oval, strong-chinned face with a long, straight
nose and large, wide-open eyes.
"Sarah Bagley. Necessity drove me to slave in
Lowell's dark, satanic mills, as
Mr. Blake so aptly would have called them.
There I discovered a talent for writing, but
could not curb enough my penchant for the
truth to satisfy the editors

of the monthly sponsored for us mill girls
by our corporate employer.
So, I departed the factory's din and choking
dust, to imbibe the odor of ink as
editor of an honest labor journal, and
agitate for the ten-hour day."
As if rapidly receding, the portrait
shrinks, the lines composing it grow
shorter and bolder. The flock draws together,
wings and bodies coalescing

into a single, solid, black dot.
Then, they explode in every direction.
Birds bewilder the blankness. Vibrating wings'
humming penetrates me from crown to
toe, like rocks purring. Clumping and parting, the
birds form words that dissolve before I can
read them. Maybe because I'm distracted by the
hopeless task of extracting verbal
sense from kaleidoscopic avian dancing, I'm
slow to get a fix on the face the

birds are composing before me, in clots and blobs
cross-hatched by inconceivably rapid,
lone fliers streaking through them, limning a
massively, grimly handsome man, his
high, broad forehead balanced on the
apex of his long, broad
nose's isosceles triangle, eyes imbued with
living fire by the birds'
constant, subtle movements, eyes that are clear,
open, undefensive, unflinching,

level, somewhat weary, alert, and steady,
riding cheeks that taper down to the
beautifully sculpted mouth's wide corners,
lips that hint at humor within, and
copious tenderness, but little cheer.
"Hi, Fred," says Victoria.
"You two know each other?" says my Zaide.
Says Victoria, "Mr. Douglass
and I were coevals in the professions of
oratory and newspaper publishing.

He, a former slave, and I, a wife,
had more than a little in common.
Also, in eighteen hundred seventy-one,
he was drafted without his knowledge
by the Cosmopolitical Party, also
known as the Equal Rights Party,
also known as the People's Party, also
known as Victoria's League, to play the
second fiddle in my race for president.
But, he never acknowledged the honor

granted him thus, as running mate of the first
female to seek that highest office."
"Madam," says Douglass, "an honor so bestowed,
even in the worthiest cause,
smacked a bit too closely of a less than
voluntary servitude.
Only my admiration for you forestalled a
disavowal, in caustic terms, of
my unlooked-for role as the first black
aspirant to second fiddle."

"When the call first sounded, in '48, to
come to Seneca Falls and proclaim the
rights of women, among the several few
men who answered, mostly husbands
dragged there by conveners, you, there of your
own impulse, were foremost, endorsing what
even some of the women were unready
to embrace – female suffrage.
We were a ticket of firsts," says V. And Douglass:
"Would that sufficient numbers of voters had

sought admission to whatever future that
ticket may have afforded them!"
Much to my relief, they laugh together.
Then he says, in the serious tones
laughing together allows, "How sad it was, in the
struggle for suffrage, that women were forced to
play second fiddle to Negro men.
I bore witness for my race, and
lost a friend in Susan Anthony. The
world demands accommodations.

Being true to oneself while holding true to
friendship, that is a great challenge.
When we rise to it, we are half the way to
heaven; when we both love and forgive
others for doing the same, we have arrived.
But, I see that you have brought my
good friend Isidor with you! Hello, Izzy!"
Zaide says, "Hello to you!
It is amusing, a mere fifty years
after they handed you the ballot,

our Victoria, if she'd still been living,
also would have been allowed to
vote for a rich, white, male goy.
So we move in baby steps."
Douglass: "Back in my day, Izzy, had there
been a few more men like you,
willing to vindicate my newly unshackled
compeers' claims on workplace justice,
I'd have loved the labor movement more."
Zaide: "Baby steps, but some day…"

Says Victoria, "Sadly, we've no time to
linger longer, if we're to bring my
loving friend to where he's meant to go
while his cheeks are pink. Delightful
though this reunion is, we must move on." The
birds disperse, unveiling the sun.
Dun yellow when half-shaded, the beach
leaps a degree towards whiteness. Its grains and
shells gleam sharply. The waves' foam
loses some detail to brightness.

Canto XIX: A Beat Cop

Overpowered by the brilliant onslaught, my
gaze quails from the blazing waters,
turning towards the clam shack, from behind which
something shapeless approaches, coiled and
glistening, like a titanium tumbleweed, a
twisting, formless form last seen in
Hell, blocking our passage, Dante's and mine.
'Hello, Bunky," I say, "when we
met below, you were somewhat dimmer,
with a hint of green." Says Bunky,

"That was then and this is now. I'm an
Angel of the Lord, and what you
saw down there, that was my Shadow." I say
"There's a Lord?" Says Bunky, "Well,
after a manner of speaking. You'll see, maybe."
I say, "Shadow?" Bunky flips a
twist of itself towards Zaide, saying, "Like this
little fella's shadow rode you
on his back, down there." I say, "Down there,
you were working security."

Bunky says, "Well, here I'm not a cop. I'm
Something that casts a cop as a shadow.
You might call me an agent of order, except the
order I'm an agent of
doesn't need no help from me to maintain it.
Even though without us on the
Force, there wouldn't hardly be no order.
This beach, in this light, the
clear light of justice, is my beat.
So to speak." "Soft gig."

"Not really." "Tell me," I say, but Bunky
interrupts me: "Back in hell,
when you wanted me to let you go where
my job was to stop you for your
own good, you asked more politely."
"Please, officer," I say, "having
thanked your shadow for oh so vividly showing
me the chlorine retching nightmares
with which it regales the souls of those whose
lives were devoted to making the means of

murder more effective and efficient,
I'd be far more purely grateful to
hear your take – an Angel's take! – on justice."
"Okay... hey! D'ya wanna see me
do the Burning Bush?" Bunky flashes
sunset red. "Thanks," I say, and
just to be on the safe side, bow. Says Bunky:
"No problemo. I yam what I yam.
I'm the One with Answers, so to speak. It
starts with, you're just undermuscled

apes with super social organization,
empathetic understanding of
anyone for whom you want to feel it, and
verbal skills just good enough so's
you confuse yourselves between what's real and
what you tell yourselves is so.
No offense. Bonobos, chimps, gorillas,
your cousins the hairy apes – and some
monkeys, too, macaques and capuchins –
like to get the short end of the

stick about as much as your grandpa does.
Baby-killers cheese off chimps.
If you're chief of a troop of chimps and macaques,
part of your job is to bust up fights that
threaten to create factions; you will weigh in
on the underdog's side, mostly.
After a scrap, a female might pick lice off
both palookas, taking turns,
drawing them closer and closer until she's got them
ready to hug and make nice.

Okay, class; now, what do we learn from this?"
I say, "Fairness isn't just for
humans. Lower primates have social rules, with
agents of order who serve and protect, and
social workers who mediate intra-group conflict."
Bunky says, "C plus. Victoria?"
She says, "Just like chimpanzees and humans,
justice and morality share an
ancestor. Long before the language evolved to
make them worthy of different names,

good and evil piqued that forebear's sense,
tuned to what a little band of
hunters and gatherers needed to hold together and
eke survival from the jungle."
"Thatta girl," says Bunky, "that's an A."
"Are you telling me," I say, "that
when I drove around Vermont, looking for
reasonable doubts the crooks who were my
boss' – their lawyer's – clients didn't do it; and
when I went to school to learn to

be like Thurgood Marshall and Gregory Peck; and
when I discovered the lovely smell of
ancient leather bindings and yellowed pages,
burning my eyes through Decennial Digests,
trawling for cases where judges who'd never heard of
me agreed with me; and when my
eyes were moist because the weeping woman
told the sentencing judge that we had
saved her life by clapping on the cuffs and
stopping her sucking fentanyl out of

hospital patients' analgesic patches; and
when I crushed my learnéd opponent
in the Second Circuit Court of Appeals; and
when, five minutes into the
jury's deliberations, defendant's counsel
asked me what conditions I might
want imposed, pending sentence; and when that
jury stunned us by acquitting; and,
when I told my clients what they could or
should not do, and what they risked by

doing or not doing as they wanted; and
when I debated my learnèd colleague
over the proper placement of a comma; and
when the waitress the chef had chased with
heavy duty meat tongs, catching her
by the breast, gave me thanks for my
services in the form of a sheet cake
frosted blue with dollar signs in
white and yellow icing adorning its borders;
are you telling me all this was

an expression of my apish heritage?"
"Now I'm gonna go biblical on you,"
Bunky says, "I'm gonna throw the Book!
Don't look alarmed. Hee hee!
We're all friends, here. So... it says that
YHWH"
(I can't reproduce what he pronounced: a
wind cat snarls and purrs)
"took the human and set him in the Garden, to
work it and to watch it, and that

YHWH
said that you must die, yes die the
day you'd eat from the Tree of the Knowing of
Good and Evil." "Tree of the *Knowledge* of
Good and Evil, you mean," I say. And Bunky:
"That's the mistranslation you got
from King James's goyish committee getting it
wrong and missing the point, as usual.
Knowledge is for apes: don't fuck your children,
don't take more than your fair share,

don't kill off the troop's next generation,
don't fight when the cops are looking,
make nice like the women tell you.
They don't think about this template,
it's just there for them, like piss and bananas.
Someday, you poor slobs may find out
if you stumbled in the right direction
when you took the path of *knowing*.
Not that long ago, your innocence was
all you had, a handful of givens, but

now that's dead to you, you have to figure
everything out with nothing much but
words to help you. *Knowing*'s a verb. Every
time you leave your corner to wrestle
with a moral question, you meet a foe that
changes and moves, and the one who rises
from the mat is someone new. You've played with
law a couple thousand years, with
legal codes, like kids who just can't learn to
do sums in their heads but have to

count on their fingers and never forget the enforcing
fists. Maybe, if the Earth don't
rise and stop your hearts, life will lead you to
need to learn to figure how to
knowingly take account of everybody's
Good and Evil, not just your own.
Maybe, that'll become a valuable skill to
teach your kids, to help them thrive.
Maybe, someone new will rise. And so, to
answer your question, yes, all that's your

human expression of your apish heritage."
"What about stupid, dishonest judges?
What about Taney, Scalia, Ciavarella?
What about lawmakers in it only
for themselves, who use the law as a club to
get what they want? Where do corrupt,
brutal police fit in?" I ask. "Two-headed
toads are born, but that don't stop the
evolution of toads. Well, maybe." Thus speaketh
Bunky, Angel of the Lord.

Canto XX: Bunky's Tiara

    Bunky flips a loop up over the tangle
    that would be its head, if it had one.
    Five triangular barbs catch iridescence
    from the sun and fling it piercingly
    at me. Bunky says, "Here are five souls,
    winking at you. Say hello!"
"Hi," I say. Says Bunky, "There, on the left –"
    "Flashing the brightest?" I ask. "Yes, they'll
each do that, when called – you knew that one. The
    parents and children of Island Pond

    won't forget how he rejected fear of
    strangers and their strange ways.
    Antithetical to the ones you named, who
    turned the law against itself,
    this judge followed the law to where it
    opens onto a greater humanity,"
Bunky declaims. I say, "Yes! I met him!
Freedom Frank, we called him. He might
    well arouse an Angel to unwonted
    eloquence!" Bunky says,

"I'm an Angel of the Lord, I speak in
all sorts of tongues." I say,
"I appeared before you once, Your Honor,
not as a lawyer but as a witness.
I don't remember and it's unimportant
why I was there, but, let me tell you, the
loneliest person in any courtroom's the witness
on the stand, all eyes on him, and
on both sides the lawyers are closing in.
Being cross-examined was just like

plucking darts from the air before they hit me. The
jury watched as if they were trying to
figure out my trick. The lawyer who'd called me
as a witness played with his pen.
In that room, only the lanky, long-haired,
black-robed guy who'd welcomed me there,
smiling sympathetically, seemed my friend.
If a man deserved to be called
Justice, it was you. But, nobody these days
gets to the highest court purely

for their love of the law. I mean, love of
law as a tool, the way a craftsman
loves a well-tuned plane or fine-honed chisel,
not for power, riches, status,
ego, thrill of combat, word games,
forced conformity, dominance, partisan
zealotry, addiction to niggling, orderly
syllogistic regularity
and the compulsion to build a procrustean bed of
it and strap humanity on it, the

moral irresponsibility of
one who merely represents –
all the seductions lawyers are prone to – but for
helping people adjust their differences
peaceably as apes, and maybe more so,
'til we can evolve a better.
Meanwhile, the least surprising thing in heaven
is that it has a place for you, in
place of the seat the Reaganite law-'n-order
vigilantes wrongly denied you.

Bunky says Island Pond buffed your luster.
So it did. And equally gleaming
was your jury instruction in <u>State v. Keller</u>,
placing the burden on the State to
prove beyond a reasonable doubt the
twenty-six defendants couldn't
reasonably have believed the only way to
get their Senator's attention
long enough to talk him out of helping the
Gipper murder Nicaraguans

was to sit outside his office until he
would agree to listen to them.
Verdict: twenty-six acquittals, and one less
Justice deserving of the name."
Bunky says, "True dat. But, let's be fair.
Some of them that rise to the top are
cream, not scum. See that next light, flashing?"
I say, "Is that Morse code?"
"D... O... J... U... S...
T... I... C... E,"

Bunky pronounces. I say, "Those words echoed
without fading from my first
day as a lawyer, when Attorney General
(as he was, then) Jeffrey Amestoy
swore me in. He tossed them off at the end,
softly, looking me straight in the eye,
so, by the way they were imparted – separate in
tone and manner from the ritual –
after he shut the book that prescribed the words I'd
raised my hand for, these lived.

As does Amestoy! What's he doing here?"
"Is your friend a little slow?" says
Bunky. "Darling," says Victoria, "biological
status has no bearing on where one
stands in what you insist, bound as you are by
chronological conventions,
on conceiving as the *after*life."
I say, "What you mean is, even
more than hell, heaven is unbounded."
"See? He comes along," says Victoria.

"We are here to upraise him, not to appraise him,"
Dante says. I'm musing on memories:
"When I returned to the office from my first
jury trial, a two-day triumph,
there were routine congratulations. After my
second, a loss, I encountered General
Amestoy in the hall by his office. Grinning,
he extended his hand to me, and
told me, 'Now, you're a real lawyer.' Of course I
loved him." "It's a happy workplace

where the patron's wise and decent, and the
workers are paid with more than money.
Such a case but instances a truth
far too large for expression by your
limited tongue, except through hints and examples,
of which, here's one: law may outgrow the
laws, but only if infused with love,
otherwise remaining forever a
sad and arid trap in which humanity
catches merely itself, and is caged."

"Yes, Victoria," Dante says, "you've touched the
reason this spark gleams so brightly on
Bunky's crown. Can the Juris Doctor
cite it for us?" I say, "Dante,
even were Bunky to spell it in neon colors,
which I sincerely hope he doesn't,
it could not be any more glaringly obvious.
Jeff, these words you authored, after
your promotion to Chief from General, stick as
fast in memory as that two-word

job description you gave me: *The past provides
many instances where the law
refused to see a human being when it
should have. The future may provide
instances where the law will be asked to see a
human when it should not. The challenge for
future generations will be to define
what is most essentially human.
The extension of our constitution's
Common Benefits Clause to acknowledge*

*plaintiffs as Vermonters who seek nothing
more, nor less, than legal protection
and security for their avowed commitment
to an intimate and lasting
human relationship is simply, when all is
said and done, a recognition
of our common humanity.* Words more beautiful
never graced a judicial decision."
Now, Bunky's crown blares a rainbow
coruscation, all across.

"Say hello to Justices Warren, Thurgood
Marshall, and Ruth Bader Ginsburg,
great expositors of your Constitution's
aboriginal intent: do unto
others as you'd have them do unto you.
And goodbye. Your time before this
court is up," says Bunky, and adds, "E voi,
mortali, tenetevi stretti a
giudicar: chè noi, che Dio vedemo
non conosciamo..." and out he blinks.

Canto XXI: Places My Morality Comes From

All my companions have disapeared, for the moment.
I look down at my hands, no longer
holding hers. Instead, a red and white
striped greasy cardboard container
occupies my fingers, and, through it, fried
clam bellies warm my palm. The
air gently licks my other palm,
cooling it as it dangles, open,
by my thigh. I ask myself, what is so
intimate as that moment one of us

moves beyond all intimacy?
Nobody answers. Here's a limit.
Just beyond what I have learned to hear,
beach grasses scratchily lengthen. I
part my lips. My tongue receives the coolness,
circles my mouth's rim: ocean's
mellow salinity, sweat's sharp tang, my
breakfast's unctuosity. Her
fragrant oils scent memory's cavern.
Ocean's tang, the forest's chemical

messages olfactory cilia capture but
lack the molecular lexicon to
reckon, add piquancy to the deep fryer's
heavy exhaust, and isn't that a
wrack of seaweed not far away?
Exquisite scratching, slowly stroking
through her bristle. Did that happen? Will it?
Limited to this moment, not a
person has an answer. Aa! Ssh.
Aa! Ssh. Aa! Ssh.

Evenly cadenced, the beach's unceasing song.
Breeze fingered leaves drone.
Seagulls khraugh! Terns wieu eu-eu-eu.
Sandpipers weet-weet-weet. My lips
purse to match their whistle. Mouths lock,
once they open. Hips open.
Open hands enmesh with open hands.
Eyes open and lock to eyes. My
lens' focus points within her black
pupil. Say what I saw through the

brilliant, ecstatic, astonishing, every-hued flash?
Not a person has an answer
limited to this moment. That's a limit.
Blue on blue, the crisp horizon,
strung between the green arms that embrace this
bay, is notched just left of center: that
snaggletooth islet the sun was kissing before I
blinked. But now, my strengthened vision
lets me stare straight into the synapse
widening between the solar fire

and the islet's tallest treetop, a hair-thin
ninety-three million miles
bringing tidings of eight minutes ago to
mingle with and enliven the various
presents I perceive in overlapping
thirtieth-of-a-second bursts that
I may recall until they peter out and
leave me to be recalled.
Don't try this at home: just as law school
taught me How To Think Like A Lawyer,

this curriculum's made me a maestro of staring.
Even so, I jerk away my
smoking retinas almost too late:
dancing scotomas veil whatever
I direct this sense towards, for a while.
Afterwards, we prolong the release of
oxytocin, I by fingertips stroking her
cheek, she by breathing into
my neck's hollow. Sooner or later,
one falls asleep: the delicate,

rhythmic hiss of a slightly congested nostril; an
eyelid's delicate, bland sweetness.
Thump and bang from back of the clam shack. The
waking city's heightened gabble of
fine particulates and gases begins to
slur the trees' clear diction.
Now it seems I've been trembling on the verge of
something that recedes behind a
blur of questions. She murmurs no answer, a
girl I knew who's become, outside my

knowing, a woman I could never know
but for having known the girl and
having had her ripped from me like a
rib and running from that loss to
losses I could be safely sure of, and why she's
here unbidden, alone with me on this
sunstruck shore, after I've let her go, to
love her, nobody's going to tell me.
That's a limit: and where shall my morality
find its beginning, if not that place from

where I kissed your eyelid, my dear heart?
(You might say, dear reader, whom I've
conjured since there's no one else to talk to,
having told you this, then I should
trace for you the system it implies, the
resolutions I would offer
to the Trolley Problem, the Drowning Child, the
Famous Violinist. To which I say,
I ain't no stinkin' philosopher! This is a poem.
You want philosophy? Get it yourself.

This, they've taught me: bullshit scenarios will not
help your reasoning find an anchor
in that place I mentioned, where there are no
binary choices. That's ass backwards.
Go there first, and reason out from there.)
While these parenthetical thoughts, which
mark my early recognition I must
bear witness to the world,
percolate rapidly through my mind, a slow
shuffle approaches from just below the

normal range of hearing, from the shack, the
sound of feet sliding through sand,
ssss sss ssss sss, limping; and,
with it, from just below the normal
threshold of scent, the stalenesses, almost rank, of an
unwashed body in unwashed clothing.
It comes closer as if through parting mists.
Yellow leather, steel-toed work boots,
deeply scuffed, with frayed, brown laces.
Cuffless, blue, khaki trousers, a

bit too long. They fold on the laces and drape the
heels, faded like the sky
near the horizon, so threadbare at the hem of
each leg wear has pulled some
feathery threads down from the crease. Skinny.
No rear end. A time-gnawed, braided,
brown leather belt, pulled tight on
almost nonexistent hips,
just barely keeps the pants from falling.
Loosely tucked in, blousing

over the belt, a blue work shirt,
worn to whitish at the wrists.
Over the left breast pocket, embroidered in
strikingly shiny golden thread,
"Peter." Long, white beard. Bushy
eyebrows. On the liver-spotted
scalp wave sparse white hairs.
Having described Peter's attire and
person with somewhat minute particularity,
I may rather annoy you, reader, by

failing to say a thing about his face. It's
not for lack of sensory competence.
Vision cleared, impressions flood all channels:
hundreds of thousands of new names
would be needed for all the scents I smell; my
skin registers wind and fabric,
barometric pressure, and humidity; I
taste my teeth and gums and saliva; the
world sings to me; my eyes delineate
every single grain of sand,

all its hollows and ridges in sharpest detail.
But, I look at his face and see the
kind of nothing you see behind your head.
Age and wisdom waft from it, and
strong benevolence. I feel like a child feels
waiting for its parent to tell it to
take its hands from its eyes and see the surprise.
Also, I feel a little nausea,
juggling what's visible and what's not. Peter says,
"It'll pass. You'll get used to it.

Anyway, you won't be here all that long." He
stabs at something on the ground with a
two-clawed trash grabber and swings it
over his shoulder – I catch a flash of
styrofoam white – into a canvas sack he
drags behind him. Where his hands should
be, or are, is another vertiginous nothing.
Peter says, "Fried clam bellies? I
like fried clams. Food of the gods. Mind you
use the trash bin, when you're done."

Canto XXII: The Malakh-Hamoves

"Who are you?" I ask. "You don't know me? Your
zaide would know me as Malakh-Hamoves.
You've met my friend Bunky, keeping the peace.
I keep a different kind of peace.
Hi, Victoria. Dante, buongiorno. You may
call me Peter. I'm wearing his shirt.
What you want to know is – " "What's up with your
hands and face?" "Yes, that, and
other things. You're seeing me just fine.
That's why I borrowed Peter's shirt,

not that he has any use for it, now.
You might find my torso upsetting.
You are not quite ready for that, yet.
When you're ready, I'll embrace you.
I'll be shirtless. It won't matter to you.
I'll receive you the way a parent
takes their newborn into their arms. That day
isn't this one. People are scared of what
brings them to me. People are scared of what they'll
look like after I've accepted them.

People are scared of my face. People are scared of
leaving behind what they leave behind.
People are scared of being left with nothing,
being left alone with nothing,
being nothing. I am nothing, to be
scared of or not, as you choose.
It will matter no more than the nakedness
into which I will receive you,
in which you will come to me forgetful of
everything but that rapt moment.

I am telling you what you want to know.
I don't know when I will hold the
last member of your species. Like you,
I do not exist and cannot
see outside the moment I occur.
Unlike you, I do not wish that
it were otherwise. You see me as you
see me, know me as you know me,
present to you through your cells that fall to
me like steady, gentle rain.

I can say what hurries homo sapiens
faster towards me. One word:
plastics. That's a joke, or maybe not.
When you've finished clogging your bodies
and your planet with immortal polymers,
you can tell me if it's funny.
Maybe you will recognize your faith in
economics based on greed and
solipsism might have been misplaced.
Maybe you will learn to wonder

how a person who can make a ploughshare
or a pruning hook instead would
make a sword or spear, and to revile him.
Maybe dumping billions of tons of
poisons on your land and crops won't seem like
it was such a good idea.
Maybe greenhouse gases will stink in your nostrils.
Maybe even cattle breeders will
learn just how unwise it is to breed
antibiotic-resistant bugs.

Maybe you will think unto the seventh
generation before you use that
new invention, even though there might be
someone who'd make money from it.
One way or another, change will end you.
Maybe DNA evolved from
yours will dance across the generations.
If you will become the creatures
who inhabit that brave new world, your fear of
me must lie down peacefully with your

understanding: I enable what's most
lasting in you to transform you;
we've made straighter, longer limbs for walking,
copious sweat glands in your scalp to
cool the brain, the flexor pollicis longus that
powers your thumb, bigger brains and
littler teeth, verbal skills, empathic
insight, guts that digest cow's milk.
Outside me, there's no salvation. You must
stop pretending I'm not there,

stop pretending I can be confined,
stop ignoring the vast machinery
you have built that massively summons me,
stop looking away from what you're
running towards, if you want to delay the
day you stumble into me.
Right now, you are offering up the
city and people of New Orleans
to my daughter, Katrina. You are preparing,
as your oily idols demand,

many more such offerings on the altars
you have made of your cities and towns.
For a creature so afraid of me,
you seem strangely devoted to drawing
us together. You think you can use me
in your little power games,
getting rid of enemies and pests as
if the world were yours alone.
I, divine and eternal, am not your tool.
Sooner or later, you are mine.

You may come to me open-eyed and slowly,
as a lover seeking knowledge
of the betrothed, or rushing wide-eyed but blind with
fear, surprised when I appear.
I don't care. For you, it makes a difference.
It might help to learn to pray.
Prayer is a form of words that, fully inhabited,
holds you in correct relation
to that part of the universe you're addressing.
Some prayers are so potent, they

elevate enormous populations.
Niklas Copernicus found himself
not the centerpiece of god's creation
as had been supposed, but riding
one of several objects around the sun,
not itself at the center, amidst a
generous sprinkling of far more distant stars.
Charles Darwin, staring at the
flow of life, found himself in it;
found me at its wellsprings;

saw nothing constant or fixed; saw that
species, his included, is no more
solid or stable than the passing clouds.
Svante Arrhenius, calculating
hecatombs of fossil fuels his species
turned to ash and gases, back in
1896 predicted warming
such as made the atmosphere a
swaddling blanket for my daughter, Katrina, her
rain, winds, and storm surges

showing what a passing cloud can do.
These are prayers that millions have heard.
It is up to you to answer them.
No, I don't distinguish between the
singular and the plural. You ask what you
might contribute to that answer.
Learn more prayers. Bend your ears to Einstein's
invocations of mass and energy,
space and time, and Bohr's and Heisenberg's hymns to
things so small they are not things.

Harken to those who yearn to reconcile the
very large with the very small,
relativity and quantum mechanics,
gravity and the other forces.
Tune your heart to Gödel's meditative
proof that no such theory can be
stated in a finite number of steps of
mathematical reasoning. Join in
contemplation Hawking's adoration
of the ultimately inscrutable.

You're a poet, skilled at indicating
nameless quiddities so precisely
any reader may feel them stir within,
though the unquantifiable mysteries
you describe can't be observed directly.
Maths and aristotelian logic
twist and crumple upon themselves before they're
near to doing what you do.
If you utter a Theory of Everything,
poetry will be its key."

Canto XXIII: Trembling On The Verge of Becoming

Without warning, my stomach plummets, pulling
all my body and limbs behind it. The
sun, that was before me on the horizon, is
overhead and rapidly growing.
I see stars, then nothing, then, again
conscious, I'm sitting on a bench, or
with the feeling of sitting on a bench,
weight on my left buttock, torso
twisted, chin resting on my wrists on
top of the bench's back, nose

pressed to the cool, glass window. So it
feels. Treetops smoothly, silently
slide from right to left, several hundred
feet below. A little behind me,
Dante and Victoria stand at attention,
dressed as flight attendants. How do I
know this? I know because I can see them, even
though they're behind me. It's less dizzying
if I watch the treetops, then our airship's
(how do I know this?) landing field as it

slowly glides to meet us, a grassy clearing a
couple of football fields in length,
sloping gently down across its width from the
wheeled wooden ramp we descend. A
few people and many wooden crates
offload with us to weedy gravel.
They can't see us, it seems. I can't see me.
If we could have brought you in body,
says Victoria (ears are not what hears her),
lingering spores of the Yellow Death

from the Time of Troubles would have killed you.
You're not immune like these folks are.
Stretched along the top edge of the field, a
red stone building startles
me by being familiar: the Billings Library,
Henry Richardson's Ruskin-inspired
gift to the University of Vermont! But,
whereas a city surrounds that gem,
here are pastures dotted with copses, sheep, and
wooden buildings with bluely gleaming,

solar-paneled roofs. Downhill, where the
lake should be, there is a lake.
Masted vessels and barges dot the bay.
Low buildings cluster around it.
Up the hill, behind Billings, a woods:
oak, maple, ash, and birch.
Me: *Where's the hospital? Where's my city?*
Where are the sounds? How did I do that?
Dante: *Burnt and razed in the Time of Troubles,*
by crusaders from Alabama

warring on the godless People's Republic. They
got the apocalypse they wanted, the
bible thumpers. Nobody lives there, now.
V: *You're here to explore. Let's go!*
Horse-drawn wagons laden with crates and barrels are
trundling down a dirt track
off the airfield's lower edge. We join them.
Wheels and horses kick up dust. It
hasn't rained here for a while. The dust
smells clean. In my nose that's

not a nose, every scent's distinct:
horses' heavy, funky sweetness;
metals, medicines, oranges, plastics' stink,
avocadoes, pineapples, peanuts;
crates' dry pine; oaken wheels'
tannic sharpness; rancid tang of
axle grease; volatile chemicals trees
broadcast to share their news; lanolin;
sheep's breath; faintly, petrochemicals.
Only halfway down the hill does

gasoline's reek roar overwhelming
from a grader smoothing the track.
HAPPY MOTHERS DAY, a dirt-smirched banner
draped over its cabin proclaims, in
blocky, red, uneven letters. The wagoners
pull to the shoulder and wave as it passes.
Near town, people cluster within a
large box alder's shade.
Like the wagoners, they wear simple clothes,
brightly dyed, resembling from a

distance a flower garden in bloom, mostly
children, but all ages, attending
to an old, white-braided woman,
square and sturdy, who supplements her
strong voice with sweeping, vigorous gestures.
Pausing, I catch her gist in a language
barely more closely akin to my mother tongue than
Chaucer's English is to American.
She's instructing them how to read the alder's
autobiography in its branches.

I am struck by her auditors' lack of fidgeting.
Briefly, a puff rustles the leaves.
When she's finished, some have questions, but I
follow a gaggle of pre-teens,
chattering, cheerful, noisy, and quick, until they
hop a fence – ignoring the gate –
into a vegetable patch. The biggest one and the
little, blonde one open a shed and
hand out half a dozen circle hoes.
All of them fall to weeding, cheerfully

chatting nonstop, not a smartphone among them.
Soon after, I'm deep in the houses.
Laid out higgledy-piggledy, oriented
so their gleaming, peaked roofs will
catch the maximum sunlight, and so the winter's
westerlies will be met by solid
walls, not glass, their windows let in morning
tinged by pastures – green, brown, or
white, with the season – while the merest loopholes
open onto the lake and, across it,

Adirondacks' blue-tinged, jagged loveliness.
Timber frame and fieldstone are the
dominant modes, but I see also turf,
cedar, slate, and houses combining
some or all of these, no two the same, a
hodge-podge of sizes and shapes, from
one-room croft to long, low dormitory.
Ridge beam ends protruding
to the riotous eaves are richly carved and
painted: flowers, leaves of oak,

maple, ash, and beech, heads of hawks,
fish, horses, deer, a cow,
intricate geometric patterns like in the
Book of Kells. A couple of kids
paint a congregation of tulips nodding
under an orange sun. The clapboards
they embellish adjoin a granite wall that
bears, in bas-relief, a tree with
many mighty branches from which dangle
tiny animals and people.

Ornamental plantings, hedges, paddocks,
vegetable plots and stands of trees
interlock like a jigsaw puzzle among the
buildings. No surveyor could have
laid out property lines so wildly squiggly.
Children play with balls and sticks, or
read, write, or draw in books, or help that
man hang laundry on a line, or
listen to that woman's stories. The air's a
field of quiet, voices distinct on it.

No electromagnetic gabble perturbs it.
Squirrels. Birds. Bugs. Breeze-stroked
greenery. Yawning cat. Distant dog.
*You've but this day here, to witness the
triumph of humanity,* Dante says.
Fear of failure freezes me.
Demographics, religions, gender relations,
race relations, class relations,
sexual mores, parenting practices,
education, economics,

politics, social control, material culture,
arts and technologies, animal
husbandry, agricultural oh my god how
can I learn enough – I can't – to
teach the who, what, where, when,
why and how of this better world?!
*All those concepts are meaningless here, or poor of
application,* says Victoria,
*here at humankind's near apotheosis,
purged of the cancerous outgrowths of greed,*

*ego, tribe, belief, and timor mortis,
trembling on the verge of becoming
something against which it cannot compete.
It would be worse than useless to preach this
future to people who are unfit to live in it.*
Dante says, *Look around, and
you will bring back home the shards of experience
that have cut their way to your heart.*
Okay, so I do not have to abandon
poetry for journalism.

Szszszsz! Szszszsz! Knowing hands guide a
plane the length of a cherry plank,
peeling curlicues that smell of fruit.
Half the workbenches lining the
tawny, well-lit room are empty. A banner
HAPPY MOTHERS DAY graces
one wall, over racks of planes and chisels.
Whirring bandsaw. Spinning lathe. A
coping saw coughs its devious path through
dark, bitter-smelling walnut.

In a barn, down the hill from the woodshop,
weavers' shuttles gently hiss
through the warp, between the beaters' thuds and
frames' clack and clatter, accreting
pick by pick their brilliant geometries. The
high ceiling, and bolts of fabric and
cones of yarn stocked deep on shelves from
floor to ceiling along one wall
soften the music. Above the southeast windows, a
valance: HAPPY MOTHERS DAY.

In a corner, a tapestry loom. On it, an
oval figure in reds, oranges,
yellows, umbers, and ochres, with some charcoal
on a field of richest blue.
After some study, I make it out to be an
evocation of a tree stump
seen from above, or a woman's genitalia.
Next door, HAPPY MOTHERS DAY is
spelled in wooden letters hanging from the
peaked ceiling's ridge beam

over the rumbling hiss of potter's wheels.
Grey lumps rise and bloom between
hands so coated with slurry they seem almost
part of what they cup and mold,
gently defining a bulbous base, then pinching and
pulling the lip to a gentle flare.
Someone drinking from this mug will kiss, with
every sip, these fingers' trace.
Now I feel I've glimpsed the heart of this place.
Back outside, a small park with

well-tended flower beds and half a
dozen children intently listening
to an adult beside a snowy hydrangea;
catty corner across the park
from the potters' shed, a refectory, where it's
HAPPY MOTHERS DAY. Near the
entrance, the heavy perfume of a soup buffet:
kimchi stew, minestrone,
chowder, dal, a rich, herby broth of
lamb with turnips, carrots, and cabbage,

next to a sideboard laden with a huge
wooden salad bowl, empty
but for a few, limp leaves, and crusty
loaves reduced to heels. Only
fragrant dregs remain in the vats. Diners
sparsely tarry at trestle tables.
Others, leaving, deposit utensils and dishes in
metal racks at the hall's far end. A
dreamy teenage boy collects them onto a
rolling cart and disappears

into a steamy, tiled back room.
I see no cashier, no bills, no
place for money to be exchanged for food.
Glossy, flame birch tables
shine like rippling, molten gold. I follow a
fat man and his skinny companion
out and downhill to a nearby, biggish structure with
plain red clapboard siding, and
follow her in. It's like a general store, but
there's no packaging, no brand names,

nothing's marked with a price, and nobody's paying.
Equally plain, the yellow-clapboarded
building next door sports above its entrance a
flagpole flying a red cross
and, you guessed it, a small banner that whispers its
crimson happy mothers day.
Hospital? Clinic? Unlike anywhere else,
lots of plastic and chemical scents.
Few patients. A man in white linens
spoons what I think is applesauce into a

little girl with a huge cast on her leg.
Is that a helipad, on the roof?
There's a shiny ambulance parked out back.
Not another car or truck.
I descend through storage sheds and warehouses,
stables, a glassblowers' workshop, a boatyard.
On the waterfront, wind turbines soar in
front of a grove of masts in the harbor.
People are disembarking. I join them, a
river flowing uphill and growing,

past the warehouses, workshops, stores (?), dwellings,
pies' brown domes cooling on
windowsills, the smell of grilling fish.
As if feeding a spreading lake, our
tributary debouches into the thousands
overflowing the Billings field
into neighboring pastures. The crowd hushes
when a man on the library's porch
plunges into chanting (microphone; speakers) a
poem, a saga, something about the

Time of Troubles and the inauguration
of a new Council of Mothers.
Seven women join him on the steps.
He hands over the microphone
to the tall, hawk-faced, black-haired one. Her
slightly raucous voice rises and
falls with an easy, flowing cadence, calling forth
laughter, then solemnity from the
crowd in equal measure. *Oh my, she's good*,
says Victoria. "On behalf of

women who have raised a child to adulthood,"
(here, I translate) "and those children,
and their fathers, and those among us whose future
runs through other people's children, and
generations we may never know the
joy of meeting; on behalf of the
land, air, and water, and all their inhabitants
visible and invisible, living by
grace of the land, air, and water, as we do;
on behalf of the web of being,

I, today elevated by you
to this Council charged with deciding
whether any proposed innovation
may rejoice or curse the future and
therefore whether we accept it, pledge my
soul to our Credo: It didn't begin with
me and it doesn't end with me." The audience
echoes this last, then breaks into song, while the
sun sets behind the mountains behind them,
splendor streaming in my 'eyes.'

Canto XXIV: A Pinpoint Spotlit Moment

With the sensation of waking, my vision returns.
I am surrounded by striped walls:
books, shelves. Then I remember climbing
red sandstone steps to here.
Then I remember picking my way through thickly
scattered bodies. Then I remember the
bodies, mostly couples, twining and moving,
sighing and moaning, making love
all across the open, grassy field.
Then I remember the crowd I was part of,

how, upon hymning the sun down behind the
distant mountains, it slowly dispersed.
Then I remember Hawk-face adjuring those who
would, to stay and bless the occasion.
I remember weeping for what we might be
and for what we are, bitterness
mixed with yearning, anger, grief, and loss.
I can't read the titles, they're blurry,
as if remnants of sleep becloud my eyes,
as if veiled by a curtain of tears.

Then I see her growing nearer, Hawk-face.
Flying towards me through the books, she
coasts to a stop before me, larger than life,
vibrant, intense. Next to her, I
feel like a beady-eyed and squeaky mouse.
"We are in her dream. She sensed us.
Now she calls us to her." That's Victoria's
beautiful voice. I see neither
her or Dante among the books. Only
Hawk-face is sharply vivid, hovering.

"Speaker, librarian, student of ancient humanity,"
Dante addresses her, "in this,
our companion, you meet one of the last
generation whose footwear caressed the
Earth before Her great fever." I say,
"That's the way he talks to a personage
whom he respects as deserving exalted status."
"Welcome, stranger. Yes, I know him,"
she says, "Did I not write, 'Dante's writings
hold the clues to most of what we

need to know about the age that birthed the
Age of Granfalloons?' And her, too,
Mother Victoria Woodhull, as we call her.
Might I know of you, my friend?"
Spoken like one who knows no enemies,
or, at least, has never feared them.
I say, "I was, or am, a lawyer turned poet,
in the city that used to be here,
in this place where you live, that the faithful,
godly, bible-thumpers razed."

She says, "Before the last of the Unitarian
steeple's ashes fell on Church Street's
cobbles, so the stories have it, a teenage
hacker from St. Johnsbury planted
malware in the Alabamans' grid,
fatally crashing it. That summer, the
heat index from Mobile to Huntsville held for
an entire lethal week at
one hundred seventy fahrenheit.
We observe three hours of silence

on the hundred seventieth day of every
year, in mourning and celebration.
Thousands of legal volumes have survived from the
Age of Granfalloons, full of
carefully worded declarative sentences and the
carefully measured verbal joinery
masquerading as reason that purports to
hold them together, but sadly, very
little poetry has, and much of that little is
very obscure, seemingly purposely."

I say, "Mister Alighieri here
taught me to speak as clearly as my
language allows, and when I've reached the limit, to
point beyond it. As for law, I
think you've nailed it." She says, "Can you help us
decrypt Ashbery, Armantrout, and
Major Jackson?" I say, "Sorry, but nope."
With the air of one who's worked an
interview around to where she wanted,
she says, "We will talk of something

153

else, then. You spoke of the 'faithful, godly'
extirpators of your community,
over whose foundations mine was built.
Faith interests us, the more so
as the Time of Troubles winnowed the world of it.
Scholarship well acquaints us with its
function of creating social cohesion through
formulae expressed with persuasive
power directly proportional to their vagueness."
"It is the substance of what we hope for, the

evidence of things unseen," says Dante.
She continues, "We are thankful
to have had it; so adults think back with
rueful nostalgia on the afflictions
adolescence suffered preparing for love; we
see from outside what used to eat us
from within, shake our heads, and try to
fathom what we barely remember,
now it's buried deep in the painful process of
learning how to age together.

You, who may have lived in propinquity with the
claimants to faith, do you preserve in
memory evidence showing its inward nature?"
I say, "I wish I could help you.
What you ask about, I've never had.
I was raised to be a citizen
of the visible world, and though at times I
questioned – as I questioned everything –
whether I might be deprived of something many,
maybe most, of the people around me

couldn't imagine a way to live without,
what I've always had to come back to is
this: the psalmist sings past my hearing.
If I'd any faith in human
progress, you might be its fulfillment, even
though I know that you are only
what your forebears bought for the price of survival.
I've seen faith, and I'm afraid my
clumsy tongue will be unequal to the
delicate task of describing it, the

little I know, but it will get tied up in
schools and cities and jobs and money and
nuclear families…" She says, "Do your best.
I have studied your texts and dug in your
ruins and kayaked through Old Manhattan." I say,
"Maybe so, but you've no notion
how flat life can be, under the thumb of a
cruel and jealous god – the dollar; that
pens its children in boxy, sterile rooms to
force-feed them the paltry skills and

lore its jealous worship requires them to
spend their lives on; where they sit in
quiet, idle rows all day and learn to
feel it not unnatural they should
pass through society only among a cohort
their own age. No wonder, some of them
bung the holes in their souls with 'truths' they grip more
tightly the more they're challenged, and fear or
pity the rest of us! I had a friend, a
little girl, brilliant, estranged by her

brilliance, creative enough so its oppression
pained her, angered at her cramped,
female prospects, torn from something important
but unknown and hidden from her.
Towards the end of our formal education,
she identified these discomforts'
source in males' violently maintained privilege."
She says, "Surely you live, if not in
hell, then near it." I say, "Telling you, it
feels as strange as those drowned streets you

paddled; under which, she rode trains. Her
gifts being coveted by the wealthy to
make them wealthier, wealthy corporations
compensated her richly for her
outlay of self on their behalf. She spent
unremunerated moments on
twenty-something female buddies, bars,
good food, wine, and clothing, and
men with whom she couldn't escape the feeling
she was behaving like a robot.

One day, over tapas, she said 'Jim, I'm
pregnant.' Then she stood there, in the
early evening light falling through her
loft apartment's view windows,
while he swept the platter and his glass of
cava to the wide-planked floor,
kneeled among the sardines and olives, banged his
fist on the coffee table, sobbing,
and demanded that she tell him how she
could have done this to him. From that

pinpoint spotlit moment of squalid emptiness,
her soul fled to the Holy Family.
Peace and meaning flooded her, receding
never, bringing refreshment and purpose.
She continued to enjoy the enjoyable
parts of her job, despising the rest,
giving her church her fullest talents, and later,
happily binding souls for eternity
with her equal in Jesus." Hawk-face says,
"What's your name? I'll look for your books."

Canto XXV: The Bird

I say, "I hope someday I will write them.
I hope, should you read them, you'll say,
here's a light that I can see by." She says,
"Yes, that would be pleasant, and useful
to me as a historian, and, to you, most
gratifying, I suppose, if
somehow you could know my gratitude."
If a person in another
person's dream can blush, I do. She says,
"Past and future are, and must be,

mutually hypothetical. Where they
intersect, joy may reside.
You are thinking, it is only in the
present where that comes to pass;
oversimple, presupposing one
present alone is all that exists.
Yes, here is a home that we can share,
long-lost older brother! Welcome!
You have twice referred to 'hope' regarding
your potential written works.

Tell me, so that I may know you better:
what is 'hope,' to you?" I say,
"One of our poets almost got it right.
She said it's a bird that never
shuts up. In the dreary hours
after dawn, before I'd wanted,
I've lain open-gummy-eyed abed,
half cursing half thrilling
to the morning chorus. Hope's like that.
I have hoped for a cowboy's chaps,

fringy vest, hat, and silver twin
six shooter cap pistols;
for the teacher please to call on me;
not to be the last one chosen;
for a puppy; for a bicycle; for the
other kids to laugh, but only
when I want them to; that my toad Skippy
wins first prize in the beauty contest;
that they won't think I'm too much a weirdo;
that I won't forget my lines;

that the rest of life won't be this lonely;
that no one will ever know;
that she'll like me; that she'll let me kiss her;
that she'll feel what I am feeling;
that she isn't frightened by my feelings;
that we'll meet again next summer;
that I suddenly, painlessly cease to exist;
that I'll draw a lottery number
so high they will never call me up;
that my first choice will accept me;

that the war will end within four years;
that the condom will not break;
that without my asking, she will tell me;
that without being told, I'll know;
that I'll understand her well enough to
know if she says yes it is for
sure the answer I will want to hear;
that I'll have enough for food,
after I have covered next month's rent;
that this job will make me happy;

that my child's good-looking, strong, smart,
honest, gentle, loved, and loving;
that my father will survive his illness;
that my mother will stop crying;
that my wife decides that she'll stay with me;
that this pain will lead to happiness;
that my child won't ever feel these feelings;
that my child will understand;
that the world will open all around to
bright and all-embracing freedom;

that the Republicans lose the next election;
that I'll do this job so well
no one guesses just how clueless I am;
that I've helped more than I've hurt;
that it was the right thing, to say no;
that we'll figure out it's really
better not to kill, abuse, and neglect, and
start to build the New Jerusalem;
that I'll say the right things to my loved ones;
that my books will find their readers.

I guess that last one could come true, now."
Dante says, "What of the hope that,
for me, 'brought true love to those on earth': the
'certain expectation of future
glory growing out of heavenly grace and
hard-earned merit.' You haven't known that."
I say, "True. I've also never seen an
ivory-billed woodpecker, but I
don't deny it might exist. Thinking
through my life list, I see hope is

hatched when desire the world will adapt to us, or
we to it, bends reason
into a hedge against fear it won't; and, nested
deep, hope sits and sings.
I can't think of anything good that ever
came to me from listening to it."
Dante says, "All hope is false that is not
grounded in a higher world than
your feet stick to." "'We are entitled
to the struggle, never the fruits,'"

Hawk-face counters. Surprised, I ask her, "Tell me
what, then, does it mean to you?"
She says, "Hope, to us, is one of childhood's
many hallucinations, conjured of
ignorant narcissism, soon grown out of.
Ask, do I mean 'childhood' only
in a literal sense, I will say no."
V. says, "In my life's first third, I
hoped my words could win for me a world of
progress, love, respect, and security.

Driven by the grand, immodest fantasy
earnest, insistent eloquence could
lend my truth what power it may need, I
soared above so many stages'
glaring footlights, raining my words into
so many hearts, until I
flew over the edge, into illness and
desperation. It might have killed me,
had a love I could not have imagined
my words had inspired, not carried

me across the Atlantic Ocean to safety
and a cherishing husband's respect." Her
gaze dazzles me, then shifts to Hawk-face, who's
laughing. Hawk-face says, "Lovely!
Lovely as the lovely giant ivory-
billed woodpecker, common now, though
north of the range from which you saw it vanish.
What a fecund world we inhabit!
Children, sensing this, conceive their hopes.
All our lives we puzzle over

potentiality – why does it sometimes seem so
limited, why does it sometimes seem to
spring on us out of the dark, why does it always
cloak itself so deep in layers of
ambiguity its essence eludes us?
Overwhelming, majestic, complex –
unexpected! Here's your future glory!"
We burst into laughter with her.
I say, "What do you call this place we both call
home?" Hawk-face answers, "Thunburgh."

Canto XXVI: Hear Me Roar

"- in commemoration of the Swedish
prophetess, one of our founding Mothers,
and the city that stood across the lake,
burnt in the Adirondack Fires, whose
people escaped on rafts to here," says Hawk-face.
I say, "When was this Swede active?
I don't know her." "What year were you born, and
what year did you come to me?"
I say, "I came into the world the year they
vaporized Elugelab and

four thousand Londoners died from breathing
London air. Now, this minute, the
Angel of Death's daughter, Katrina, is drowning the
Crescent City. Has she made her
mark, yet?" Hawk-face says, "By then, the
only marks she'd made were on her
parents' clothes, with baby spit-up. Wait a
dozen years, until another
greedy, ignorant, witless, psychopathic
liar is your Commander in Chief.

Then, you'll hear our Mother Greta roar."
Snaps alight beside her a slim
wand, glowing white as a sabbath soul, so
bright it would be painful to look at
out of ordinary eyes. Says Hawk-face,
"Thus illuminates each
generation the ones that came before it."
I say, "Do you mean by shedding
light on the past, or by spitting up on it?"
She says, "Both." Laughing, we are

much less strangers. But, the wand is silent.
I say, "I am honored to meet a
spirit honored as you are, and I intended
no offense," petering out as
slowly an indulgent, affectionate smile
blooms on Victoria. She says, "That is
not Ms. Thunberg. It's the dreamer's image
of her. What, you wonder, will or
did she do to merit veneration?
She was a child, and will be a child.

In her childish truthfulness, she'll shame the
leaders of nations to their faces
for their dereliction of the primal
human duty to care for children.
Shaking with passion, she'll proclaim to them a
child's need, a child's right, to
feel and know that it's safe and will be protected.
On them, like a tongue of flame, will
play her anger at their pursuit of money and
fantasies of endless growth while

what's in store are drought, flood, and pestilence.
Did she scorch them into shame?
She'll be loved for asserting the claims of love."
Hawk-face: "Evolution's gift, this
love it devised to facilitate itself, a
gift for itself and not for us, in
which it allows us such a share of pleasure."
Dante: "Yes, God is good!"
His ejaculation, sweetly earnest,
almost astonished, almost pleading,

sparks more laughter. Because this is a dream, I
am particularly conscious
how the cushions of my lips gently
meet upon my merriment's closing,
and how, when they peel apart again, the
voice they issue is not my own:
"Arkhipov, at your service." Hawk-face says,
"Here for you to study, my friend, a
spirit – not an image! – somewhat less
pure than Mother Greta, therefore

maybe easier for you to relate to.
That power, which moved them both,
moves our conjunction, and animates
Councils such as the one I lead.
Admiral, tell us your story, please!" Do I,
at the ensuing appropriation of
all my organs of speech, feel myself a
helpless victim of horrid puppetry?
No. It seems so perfectly natural, that this
history comes through me as mine,

told in Russian, a language I don't know:
"I was commander of a flotilla,
four Soviet diesel submarines
ordered from the Arctic Sea to
secret tropic stations, near to Cuba.
You should know, the year before,
I was executive officer on the first
nuclear powered submarine the
Soviet Union hastily threw together to
answer America underseas.

On her maiden voyage, this K-19
blew a reactor coolant pipe.
Engineers, at Captain's orders, cobbled
water pipe to air vent,
patched the system, and avoided meltdown.
Inside a month all eight
engineers died unpleasantly,
buried at sea in lead-lined caskets.
They were sacrificed because our Captain
feared exploding reactor might damage a

nearby NATO base in Greenland, triggering
full-scale nuclear missile exchanges.
I was much impressed by these events.
Now, four weeks after launching in utmost
secrecy, I wait for orders that do not
come, in Sargasso Sea, in boat that was
built for frigid northern waters. Here, the
surface is warm as a bath you could soak in, so
long as you poked only your nose above it.
Enemy planes and ships force us

to remain submerged for lengthy periods,
surfacing only to charge our batteries,
only at night, unless we cannot wait.
Air-conditioning fails. Amidships, the
engine compartments reach sixty celsius.
Crew take breathers fore and aft,
gasping at forty – a hundred fahrenheit.
Drinking water's rationed: quarter
liter per man per day. Luckily, we are
oversupplied with fruit compote.

Stink of diesel and sweaty, unwashed men.
Skin breaks out in rashes, open
sores, infections. Nausea, fatigue, confusion,
headaches, dizziness from air not
scrubbed of carbon dioxide. Men faint,
even on duty. Sleep's elusive,
brief, and unrefreshing. We're spotted! We dive, with
six hours charge in batteries.
Nothing from Moscow. Florida radio tells us:
Russians are manning Russian missiles

based on Cuba; Cuba's blockaded; Kennedy's
organizing an airborne invasion;
Kennedy's warned Americans, don't be surprised
if atomic bombs start flying;;
in the state of Florida, they're constructing
prison camps for Russians; a diplomat
posted to Cuba just before the death of his
wife isn't allowed to return to
Moscow so that he could attend her interment.
We are alone, to add it up.

Now, they drop depth charges around us.
It's like sitting in a metal
barrel someone's constantly blasting with a
sledgehammer; someone who doesn't know their
hammer might be answered by nuclear warheads
on the tips of torpedoes we don't
need an order from Moscow to fire, if all
officers in command agree.
Four hours of this. Batteries drained, we're
running on emergency lights, and

now, the strongest blast so far. How much
more her hull will take, who knows?
Captain Savitsky erupts. 'Maybe war has
already started up there!' He orders to
'ready special weapon' and bellows, 'We're going to
blast them now! We'll die, but we'll sink them!
We will not disgrace our Navy!' Political
Officer Maslennikov nods his head.
I am looking at them and thinking, maybe,
Valentin Grigorievich,

you guessed right and everyone we know is
dead already; maybe, comrade
Captain, war is waiting for us to start it.
It's like Schrodinger's Cat, you know, the
cat is closed in a box, you don't know is it
dead or alive until you raise the
lid, but when you raise the lid you'll maybe
trigger something that kills the cat.
Maybe they're playing cat and mouse with us.
Maybe they're signaling, come to surface.

Maybe they're boxing us in while they await their
final orders to finish or spare us.
Maybe if we never open the box, the
cat won't know what happens to it.
I don't know. I can't think straight. I am
tired and sick and everything is
pissing me off, including you, my little
Captain. I just want to stop it.
So do you, my brother. But we have duties and
large responsibilities.

I command this flotilla. On this boat,
three yeses are needed. You do
not have mine, unless you prove that when you
open the box, cat will meow. I
told you, I'm not thinking clearly, not much
more than you are. This, I know.
Next grenade could crack us open, maybe.
Any decision may lead to disgrace, but
only one will bring us to fresh air and
maybe someday to see our loves."

Canto XXVII: Gentle, Motionless Arms

Hawk-face sings, beginning with the hymn that
moved me so on the lawn in the sunset.
Other voices join her, bringing other
tunes, a slow, harmonic welding,
reminiscent sometimes of fugal twinings,
sometimes of Dixieland's conversational,
barely contained, consensual anarchy, sometimes of
female Balkan choirs whose discipline
comprehends the logic and need of breaking
into occasional yips and screeches,

all at once expressing joy and sorrow,
fiercely beautiful, raw, and human.
Sometimes, having closed your eyes to listen,
music takes you so far into
its own dream that all your other senses
leave the sleeper alone in the room,
gently shooing each other out, and only
tip-toe back when the sound recedes.
So, I languidly allow my portals
to reopen and focus. Hawk-face

fountains forth a ruddy radiance twice as
bright as the orange, yellow, green,
blue, indigo, and violet blazes
fanning out to either side of her.
She says, "Welcome, friendly pilgrims! What you
heard just now is how we open
our council's meetings. We have questions.
Flesh and blood of our flesh and blood,
predecessor in spirit, attentive one,
lover and servant of language, that which

hides in language, and that which language hides,
careful observer, faithful reporter,
officer of your courts, sworn to an ethics
based on truth's emergence from conflict,
by the oaths that your existence swears to
ours and as you'd have your children
know your struggles, can you, or your peers to
whom you'll return, give answers
that will help us comprehend your people's
choice to live so that the lesson

you taught us was not to be like you.
Even the birds whose brains you derided
know the truth we teach our children, not to
let their feces foul their nests.
When and why did you forget that? When and
why did an abstraction, money,
so distract you from the skills and knowledge
of survival it became your
measure of success and means to power?
Having tethered yourselves to something

nonexistent outside yourselves so fully
it determined all important
choices, blinding you to externalities
(as the real world costs were
euphemistically categorized by even
those clear sighted enough to see them),
why did you ignore or fail to perceive that
you were adapting yourselves to nothing?
Did you think you'd made the earth irrelevant?
Where, if not there, did you think you lived?

Why did you proudly, enthusiastically rush to
kill and be killed on behalf of
territorial administrative units and
other purely conceptual entities?
When the drowning cities' refugees were
dying of thirst among you, the burning
croplands' dispossessed fainting with hunger,
why did you share with them only squabbles
over usufructuary rights?
Why did you let the minds impaired by

wealth and status, leached of generosity,
dulled to empathy, self-absorbed,
be your alphas? Why did you knowingly stride
up to and over cliff after cliff like
ruminants being herded to slaughter, when the
only ones herding you were you?
Do not try to tell me. I ask so you
know what questions you'll leave behind."
Dante: "E tu, figliuol che per lo
mortal pondo ancor giù

tornerai, apri la bocca, e non
asconder..." I say nothing.
Says Victoria, "He is mute with sadness."
Hawk-face: "When I awaken, and he's a
harshly interrogated memory finding
its new place in the past, he will
open his eyes on a sunlit beach, the ocean, the
country rising behind him, the creatures
that inhabit them and the sky above, and
he will find not only some small

joy in his own life, but also the memory
after so much pain of happier
people living sanely with the planet.
What he says, then, may encourage
that new era through its birth pangs,
like a husband whispering 'push'.
Even if his words have no more impact
than a single flutter of a
buddhist prayer flag, they'll be holy."
I say, "I have never had much

use for holiness such as I saw around me,
but, in the sense you give it, I will
give my life to it." WHOOSH! Exploding
into brilliant profusion, the chorus
flares, flinging tendrils and gouts of light!
Filaments branch, proliferate, ramify,
loop, and tangle faster than time-lapsed beanstalks.
In a blink, the space is enjungled.
Piercing luminosity envelops
us, as if we're rolled in a floral

pattern fabric woven of laser beams.
I am stunned. Victoria says,
"Breathe. Breathe, and accept her happiness."
Stripped away long ago, if
only days ago, my defenses against
anyone else's deepest emotions
penetrating past my intellect, I
bathe, a long, soaking bath,
feeling myself dissolve to a core of something
floating like a yellow rubber

duck in the gentle, motionless arms of her light.
Hawk-face: "We have a word for the times that
rooted and fed you, and all the civilizations,
so called, from our species' earliest
urban coagulations, small as the spots on a
petri dish, to the Time of Troubles:
Ozymandias; in its latter part, the
Age of Granfalloons, when decadent
Ozymandias devolved into demographic
dislocations, massive destruction of

infrastructure and institutions, death by
thirst, hunger, war, and disease, and
heightened exposure to all of survival's exigencies.
No person was unaffected.
In this morass of its own corruption and filth,
Ozymandias generated
many variations of human society,
formed from what the decaying corpse
left for them to build with, local resources,
climate, and what kind of luck they

had in their neighbors, vying ferociously over
clean water and arable land.
Aping the formerly dominant stock, some,
well adapted to swim in cesspools,
wielded and temporarily retained those
powers rooted in toxicity.
By no measure were the Troubles brief.
We emerged from Ozymandians
who'd developed resistance to that era,
outcompeting those who failed to

recognize the game had changed, that cruelty,
riches and violence trumped no longer
mutual aid and cohesion of psychologically
whole, stable, resilient, adaptable
individuals bonded by understanding,
need, love, and affinity.
Holy! Holy! Holy! Holy! Holy!
as your poet wrote, and in your
own way you may echo." I say, "What do you
call yourselves?" She says, "Us."

Canto XXVIII: Antiphonal Hymn From the Crystalline Sphere

Us! Us! Us! Us! Us!
Waves lapping sandy beach.
Holy! Holy! Holy! Holy! Holy!
Breakers curling, foamy surf.
Us! Us! Us! Us! Us!
Waves lapping sandy beach.
Holy! Holy! Holy! Holy! Holy!
Breakers curling, foamy surf.
Us! Us! Us! Us! Us!
Waves lapping sandy beach.

Susurrus of us! of us! of us!
Marking the moment of stasis before it
slides back and into itself, the water
leaves a scalloped line on the sand.
Holy! Holy! Holy! Holy! Holy!
Breakers curling, foamy surf.
Susurrus of us! of us! of us!
Marking the moment of stasis before it
slides back and into itself, the water
leaves a scalloped line on the sand.

Susurri are us! are us! are us!
Each terminal moment erases
segments of earlier lines, creating a line of
lines of many termini.
Holy! Holy! Holy! Holy! Holy!
Breakers curling, foamy surf.
Susurri are us! are us! are us!
Each terminal line erases
segments of earlier lines, creating a line of
lines of many termini.

Suss! Suss! Suss! Suss! Suss!
Every so often, one wave
washes the sand, erasing all traces
but its own, wavy mark.
Holy! Holy! Holy! Holy! Holy!
Breakers curling, foamy surf.
Suss! Suss! Suss! Suss! Suss!
Every so often, one wave
washes the sand, erasing all traces
but its own, wavy mark:

Suss us! Suss us! Suss!
arcs composed of bubbles,
strings of foam, tiny shells, the border
separating wet from wetter,
Holy! Holy! Holy! Holy! Holy!
Breakers curling, foamy surf.
Suss us! Suss us! Suss!
fish bones, bits of weed,
quartz dust, six pack rings,
colorful shreds of nylon rope;

Us! Us! Us! Us! Us!
Waves lapping sandy beach.
Holy! Holy! Holy! Holy! Holy!
Breakers curling, foamy surf.
Us! Us! Us! Us! Us!
Waves lapping sandy beach.
Holy! Holy! Holy! Holy! Holy!
Breakers curling, foamy surf.
Us! Us! Us! Us! Us!
Waves lapping sandy beach.

Susurrus of us! of us! of us!
faint, ephemeral traces drawn by
water on a granular mineral substrate
permeated by salty water.
Holy! Holy! Holy! Holy! Holy!
Breakers curling, foamy surf.
Susurrus of us! of us! of us!
Faint, ephemeral traces drawn by
water on a granular mineral substrate
permeated by salty water.

Susurri are us! are us! are us!
Draining through jaggedy interstices, it
washes roly polys, sand crabs,
beetles, hoppers, blood worms.
Holy! Holy! Holy! Holy! Holy!
Breakers curling, foamy surf.
Susurri are us! are us! are us!
Draining through jaggedy interstices, it
washes roly polys, sand crabs,
beetles, hoppers, blood worms.

Suss! Suss! Suss! Suss! Suss!
Swash and backwash, they scud, hop, and
swim, seeking things to eat, avoiding
desiccation and death by drowning.
Holy! Holy! Holy! Holy! Holy!
Breakers curling, foamy surf.
Suss! Suss! Suss! Suss! Suss!
Swash and backwash, they scud, hop, and
swim, seeking things to eat, avoiding
desiccation and death by drowning,

Suss us! Suss us! Suss!
up and down the intertidal
zone, where time articulates itself in
cycles of pulses of water. Cycles
Holy! Holy! Holy! Holy! Holy!
Breakers curling, foamy surf.
Suss us! Suss us! Suss!
pulled by the moon and pulses driven by
airborne solar energy beat the measures
lives rise and fall within.

Us! Us! Us! Us! Us!
Waves lapping sandy beach.
Holy! Holy! Holy! Holy! Holy!
Breakers curling, foamy surf.
Us! Us! Us! Us! Us!
Waves lapping sandy beach.
Holy! Holy! Holy! Holy! Holy!
Breakers curling, foamy surf.
Us! Us! Us! Us! Us!
Waves lapping sandy beach.

Susurrus of us! of us! of us!
Some wait for night's safety to
pick fly larvae off rotting seaweed.
Some eat plankton the waves brought.
Holy! Holy! Holy! Holy! Holy!
Breakers curling, foamy surf.
Susurrus of us! of us! of us!
Some – detritivores – subsist on
life's leftovers. Some scour the sand for
food. Some eat each other.

Susurri are us! are us! are us!
Also on the menu: algae,
and bacteria by the tens of thousands
hiding in every sunless sand grain's
Holy! Holy! Holy! Holy! Holy!
Breakers curling, foamy surf.
Susurri are us! are us! are us!
nooks, like alpine valley villages.
Mountains wear away. Earth grinds them.
Then it sweeps the debris to beaches.

Suss! Suss! Suss! Suss! Suss!
There, beneath the slightly inclined
plane of sand, salt, and water sheening
in the morning sun, these lives,
Holy! Holy! Holy! Holy! Holy!
Breakers curling, foamy surf.
Suss! Suss! Suss! Suss! Suss!
manifestations of the law
quod existit, cohaeret and its force that
aggregated primordial elements

Suss us! Suss us! Suss!
in the bellies of stars whose dead and
shattered remains then coalesced, bringing us
carbon, nitrogen, phosphorus, sulfur,
Holy! Holy! Holy! Holy! Holy!
Breakers curling, foamy surf.
Suss us! Suss us! Suss!
will outlast us. Here he stands,
just where the last swash tickled his toes,
lifting a fried clam to his mouth.

Canto XXIX: If You Want To See It, There It Is

It's so odd to see oneself from this height, as
if the camera had zoomed way out.
There's that little guy, wetting his toes. The
whorl in his hair at the back of his head
spirals like the arms of the Milky Way.
Floating up here beside me, angelic
with her wavy, dark hair, shining
eyes, and white linens billowing,
V says, "Dante wants to tell you a fable."
I say, "Tell him, I'm always listening."

Dante says, "Once upon a time, there
was a place that, the older it got, the
larger and larger it got, faster and faster.
Things within it, themselves enlarging,
kept on growing farther and farther apart.
Explanations abounded. Some said,
'It is creation's love for the love that gives it
being, feeding back like Jimi
Hendrix's Star Spangled Banner at Woodstock,
making ever more of itself.'

Others preferred elucidations within the
limits numbers might express.
Be that as it may, this much was certain:
it was the nature of this place to
grow more and more, filling with emptiness."
I say, "Did you really reference
Jimi Hendrix, just now?" "Poetry's timeless,"
he says, "and I see him, peering
at me, in the eye of god. If that's not
fourteenth-century-ish enough, then

I can't help you. Shall I continue? Yes:
it was like the chest of a singer
caught inhaling forever between notes.
Maybe the place's essential expansiveness
carried these corollaries: something held the
objects randomly sprinkled throughout it
separate, individual, segregated,
no two able to occupy the
same space simultaneously; but,
clinging together, reaching over the

most enormous distances to each other,
tighter embracing the closer they came, the
more massive the hugger, the firmer the hug.
No: on second thought, don't think of
arms affectionately grasping elbows,
drawing close a loved one.
Everything emanated omnidirectional
yearning for everything else, more like.
Waves of yearning pervaded the place, ripples
of it criss-crossed, weakening farther

from their sources but never disappearing,
nowhere exempt from existences falling
for whatever anywhere also exists:
dust, asteroids, comets, moons,
planets, stars, nebulae, galaxies, clusters.
At the start, and long thereafter,
it was easy for them to hold each other.
Although inexorably distance
forced itself between them, smidge by smidge,
even as they, too, swelled,

for the nonce they had the strength to deny it.
Here and there, consciousness blinked.
Whirling in acrobatic, elliptic routines,
things collided, struck off shards that
caromed into the ceaselessly bloating, relative
emptiness, finding other things to
hit or orbit. A trapeze artist's grip may
tire and slip a partner's wrist;
so, in time, these structures of mutual embrace
loosened, lengthened, relaxed to the merest

fingertip brushes easily swished away by
almost any perturbation.
Structures evaporated. Finally, only the
hitherto irreducibly smallest
bits remained intact. Their integrity
held against annihilation
stronger the more attenuation pulled at it.
This was a long, invisible struggle.
Prying energies exhausted themselves,
sweating out short-lived contradictions.

Is that not like love? At last, it was the
place itself that undid them. They could
withstand any physical violence (short of a
black hole) that may strike from
any of the six directions, but not
all directions pouring infecund,
unremitting increase into their being,
ineluctably magnifying and
breaking their selfhood with infinite sudden ferocity,
tearing them apart, blasting their

shattered, disintegrated remains, hot by
ten to the thirty-second power,
into bubbles blown in spacetime's membrane,
baby universes winking
on all over like Christmas tree candles,
each uniquely manifesting
condensates derived from their voided source.
Most burn out. Some, like
this our home, survive for a while." He pauses.
After waiting for him to resume,

I say, "If it's a fable, what's the moral?"
He says, "If you want to see it,
there it is, and if you don't, there's none."
I say, "Makes me think of the mists that
once a year shroud coral reefs, the
maples' helicopter samaras
whirligigging down each spring, the millions of
sperm that race to every egg."
He says, "That's the way a poet thinks,
talking cosmology, hearing sex."

I say, "As my zaide might have said, 'a
kluger hert eyn vart, aun farshteyt
tsvey.'" And he replies, "Okay, smart guy.
Seven hundred years ago, I
told you each and every of the countless
members of God's creation is differently
constituted to receive His love;
and, that single Source illumines
from behind your strongest telescope's reaches
every moment, every where."

Canto XXX: Lushens, Engreening

There I am, a morsel poised at my lips.
Suddenly, like a blinding squall,
living light surrounds me, so thickly
nothing can get through it to me.
Just as quickly, my eyes adjust, and I am
here, a morsel poised at my lips,
millions of Blake's worlds under my feet,
air warmed by my body
rising in a convective sheath around me
and a thermal plume above me

wafting skywards the moisture and odors of me.
"Like a censer," whispers Dante.
Previous embodiments were shocks.
Birth was the roughest. Pain and delight
flowed in equal measure through that opening
to the simultaneous demands of
gross motor coordination and consciousness.
This, by contrast, is more alike to
slipping into a supple, silken stocking.
So smooth! But, I can't tell you,

telling some of it one word at a time,
what it is to feel and to know
what I'm feeling and knowing all at once.
Perspiration feeds and waters
billions of tiny lives that colonize my
skin, keeping intruders at bay.
They accept the integument they ride on
thoughtlessly, not much more so than do
we the crust that feeds us, only a bit more
ignorant of what's within it

than are we of earth's seething heart.
Let me praise, then, since I have the
words for that, at least, if not much more, the
infrastructure engineered by
millions of years of time and chance to form me,
firm me, shield me, support me, guide me.
Praise my skin, within its skin of air, and the
skeletal frame it stretches over.
Praise the hidden marrow, yellow and red.
Praise the sensory systems of which I

am but intermittently aware
(ordinarily) and have no
names for but the five I recognize as
sources of reliable data
even as input from all of them informs my
every movement and operation.
Praise my intricate web of tendons and muscles.
Praise the complex series of processes
that reduce tissues left by formerly
living plants and animals such as the

fried clam that yielded so delightfully
to my teeth and tongue just now,
starting its disintegration into
thousands of individual chemicals,
separating out the toxic and useless,
allocating and transporting the
useful wherever they may be most needed,
independent of my will.
Praise my lungs, their movement and acceptance
of the air's offer of goodness.

Praise my heart, whose nature is never to rest.
Praise the autonomous, multiple chemical
and electrical feedback and messaging systems
that from minute to minute minutely
regulate my inner operations.
Praise my liver. Praise my kidneys.
Praise my constant protection by multiple layers of
weapons and agents, including friendly
aliens populating my skin and guts,
ranks of cells that search and destroy, that

signal alarms, that make and deliver toxins,
under command and control systems
that direct production, transport, deployment,
burn the enemy with fever,
flood the battlefield with mucus, encyst,
clot, rebuild, knit, heal.
Praise this persistent collaboration among
thirty-seven trillion native
sharers of my DNA and a roughly
equal number of fellow travelers,

over which a vast network, in its
densely compacted interconnectedness
the most complex object known to itself, a
flabby, grey lump, proudly
stakes its exclusive claim and presumes to preside.
Praise that erstwhile seat of my being.
Praise the machinery, dormant just for now,
with which I'm equipped to render
unto another my moiety of the molecules
we will need to complete the project

we are primed for beyond all other purposes.
Praise that seat of my being, too.
Praise in the highest degree, bearing in mind
choices I have made, for the long,
slow, incremental creation of species
one from another; for its invention of
what we recognize in ourselves as volition; for
keeping those mortal powers confined to
such a tiny sphere, at first, of choices –
whether to pounce or crouch in waiting,

run or freeze, fight or flee, mate or
seek another, play or rest; for
making us the creatures of our own,
slightly larger sphere, a marble,
still, beside the involuntary moon, but
one we may enhance with careful
training and meditation, if only a bit, and
learn what differences doing so makes.
I see grass sprouting from the sand.
Thin, to begin with, as the hair on an

old man's scalp, it rapidly thickens,
lushens, engreening into a weedy,
shaggy, ripe for mowing, backyard lawn.
It's the patch behind my house.
There in the corner's the scraggly arborvitae
overshadowed by buckthorn saplings.
Lying near it, a thing the length of my forearm, a
grey streak on the creeping charlie.
Stepping cautiously closer, I see it's a rabbit.
Why is it lying there, so still?

Then I see it's breathing, and I see the
straight, clean slash that opens its
belly front to back, revealing a jumble of
lilac, lavender, brown, and yellow
organs, still tightly packed and glistening.
Did a hawk do this, then drop you?
As I bend a little closer, you scrabble
with your stiff front legs, dragging your
shoulders to interpose your head between
me and your body, fixing on me an

eye's expressionless, dark blue bead.
I retreat to the shed for a spade to
end this misery, but, when I return, the
rabbit's dead. I bury it.
Hanging the spade back on its peg, I'm followed
by your dark blue bead
and the strength that utterly spent itself on
facing whatever I might bring you.
Gyres in darkness a bead as blue as the ocean
I face in my shock and awe.

Canto XXXI: In Which We Meet Some Special People

Once again, my eyes are filled with water,
sky, sun, and the tawny strand.
"Where's Victoria?" I ask, looking around.
"Over there," says Dante, pointing.
While we were wherever we were, the beach was
filling with people, not a solid
mass like that which clogs the Burlington waterfront
every Fourth of July, more like
jimmies sprinkled on a frosted cupcake,
sparsely enough so there is space to

easily navigate among them and for
lines of sight to penetrate,
avenues that randomly open and close with traffic
currents and people's Brownian motion.
So, the crowd is loosely woven, an airy,
gauzy, celebratory banner
flapping in breezes of its own making.
Here we are, in the highest heaven!
How I know that's where I am, I don't know,
but I know that knowing I'm there is

my most certain clue, and part and parcel
of the fact of being here.
Josephine Baker, flaunting ostrich feathers,
capers around a circle of drummers.
John Lennon beats an enormous djembe.
Standing shoulder to shoulder, Beethoven
and a red-haired priest play interlocking
tootles on Peruvian pipes.
Focusing on Ms. Baker's feet, I notice,
when she touches down between her

leaps, they don't compress or scatter the sand.
Likewise with the conga line that
follows her, exuberantly threading the
smiling, slowly milling throng.
Nobody's feet sink into the sand, but mine.
Gaily waving a handkerchief, the
last dancer – "Henry James?" I ask, and
Dante answers, "Yes, and he is
holding hands with Tilman Riemenschneider" –
disappears behind a knot of

celebrants, clearing the path to a view of Victoria
maybe a hundred feet away
chatting with an elderly couple whom, the
same moment the view closes, I
recognize. "It's Mom and Dad!" I gasp.
"Go to them. What are you waiting for?"
Thus urged by Dante, I hesitate.
"I see something odd. I want to
see it clearly before I take the plunge,"
I say. "Bless you," Dante says.

I had glimpsed the faintest, silver-blue,
flickering glints among the crowd,
hints of luminosity, barely discernible
over the strengthening morning light.
Watched for several hundred heartbeats, the vision
stabilizes. Flickers thicken
into pulses of something rarefied, subtler
than the stuff my lungs pump,
bathing the beachgoers head to toe. Concurrently,
they, who'd first appeared to me

solid as underarm stubble, slowly translucify,
little by little attaining a limpid
lambency like theatrical lighting gels
glowing from within. I say,
"I am seeing things I have no names for."
"Bless you," Dante says, "and may you
soon begin to feel them, too." Still, I
hesitate, unsure I'm ready.
Having struggled, late into adulthood,
to perceive those two as simply

people like myself, it's jarring to find them
elevated once again,
beings much more luminous than the beacons
my youth took its bearings from.
Will the joy I worked so hard for, of seeing them
plain, be retrospectively shrunk to the
mere dimensions of my own satisfaction?
Like an optometrist clicking through her
lenses, I shift my perception. Now, the partiers
look like normal, happy people.

Now, high spirits, gently glowing, play and
plash in ethereal currents. Now,
millions of bugs, birds, and other critters.
All equally large as life.
Reassured, I enter the light-footed throng, my
every step an eager trudge. I
pause beside a volleyball net, a spectator.
Six elderly men play. They're
aerial as Josephine Baker. Unexpected,
gentle tones address me from a

spot some inches above my ear and several
feet behind me and to my left.
"May I introduce my friends to you?
Please say hello to Muhammad Ali,
Bill Russell, John Carlos, Tommie
Smith, Karim Abdul Jabbar, and
Colin Kaepernick. Their brave insistence on
decent treatment for humans, as such,
elevated every person a tiny
baby step closer to heaven.

So, while life is in them, their spirits play here."
Turning, I see a tall, slender
man in a cardigan, white shirt, khaki
slacks, and very clean sneakers.
In the distance over his shoulder, I watch a
rope of heavenly fluid wrap in
coils around a ballerina's waist – I
know she's a dancer by her tutu –
then, as if whipping a dreidel into motion, it
swiftly uncoils. She twirls en pointe to the

volleyball players, embracing one like a lover.
"Anyone may get lost in wonder,"
says the man, fixing his penetrating,
kindly, inquisitive eyes on me.
I move on in search of Victoria and my
folks, my new companion beside me.
His immaculate Keds don't stir a grain.
Neither of us says a word.
Speaking feels superfluous, for now.
We are passing a tall, thin,

elderly woman dressed in blue jeans and a
black and gold Saints t-shirt, who
stands erectly by the water, scanning the
passing crowd, when she calls out,
"Where is my son?   Have you seen my son?"
Calm unbroken, my friend hastens
to her, trailing me. Her face is wet.
Telling our names, he asks for hers.
She says, "Maryam. I am yet an exile
and a stranger in this place.

My son got up on the roof and slipped and
fell and then there was no one to
help me climb out from the waters. So, I
come to beach among the blessèd
from an attic apartment on Tennessee near
Claiborne in the Lower Ninth,
to eternity from time,
from America to a people
just and sane." She falls to her knees, sobbing.
My companion, who called himself Fred,

kneels beside her, forehead to forehead, hand on her
back between her shoulders, until her
wracking eases. They whisper together a while.
Then he rises and silently leads me,
I assume towards where I want to go.
Soon, we approach a lifeguard tower,
topped with a huge umbrella painted to look like a
lotus, surrounded by the densest
throng I've seen here, many holding burning
sticks of incense, faces upturned

towards the tower's top, where sits a small
skinny man in saffron orange
speedos, mirrored shades, and an orange t-shirt.
On the left, above his heart,
in blue thread, a name's embroidered: "Sid."
He reclines in his wooden chair,
head held level as if he's contemplating
everything before him, utterly
clear, a coruscating fountain of colorless
light so brilliant he's hard to see.

Canto XXXII: Nice Shot, Susan!

Fred says, "Please say hello to my friend, Siddhartha."
I emit a starstruck stammer.
I've forgotten whatever words comprise it
even before I've spoken them.
Leaning over the railing, he says, "You can
call me Sid," and doffs his shades.
"People always want to find out what I
really look like," he says, but even
using the lens that focuses on particular
facial characteristics, he's vague:

handsome, but not enormously so; maybe a
little like Roshan Seth, the actor;
maybe a little like Apu, from The Simpsons;
wholly (through the lens with which I
saw him first) a sunlight-bursting diamond.
"Thank you for your service," I say.
Seeing that I'm tongue-tied, he sighs, and says,
"Thanks for visiting. Come back, anytime.
Maybe next time we can talk." Nodding
vigorously, dazed with dazzlement,

I move on with my guides in search of Victoria
and my parents, whom I've glimpsed
farther away than at first. It seems the beach is
growing fuller. Maybe that's why
it seems bigger. "All these heavenly people!
Who are they?" I ask. "Well, Maryam,
back there, raised up seven children, mostly
by herself. They grew up peaceful,
kind, and loving. Only her second oldest
stayed in town, employed as a janitor

in an elementary school. He lost that
job a month before the storm.
Neither he nor Maryam owned a car.
They could not evacuate.
He went to her home to help her. They had
just decided to shelter at the
Superdome, and then the levee broke."
I am silent, contemplating
what I have been told about this flood, its
cold black water the converse of

our surroundings. Fred continues, "Most of the
people here, like Maryam, are here
due to their love, patience, and understanding for
children who were in their care.
That's the problem with these tours, they focus
too much on the famous folks.
Probably, you have never heard of the village of
Nieuwlande, in the Netherlands, or of
any of its inhabitants during the Nazi
Holocaust, but they're all here.

So are all the French who stuck their necks out,
vulnerable as geese, hiding Jews in
wartime Le Chambon-sur-Lignon.
Pretty name! 'Rosenstrasse'
is another pretty name, beautified
by the wonderful courage of German
women who gathered there in the winter cold of
nineteen hundred forty-three, in the
name of love and on behalf of loved ones.
They are all here, too, and all the

Danes who chose to wear the yellow star.
In the land of Israel, some Jews –
sadly, few – have found their way to here through
olive groves. At harvest time, they
interpose their bodies between the trees and the
bulldozers, fire, spades, and axes of
people with hurtful intentions towards their neighbors.
In the future, some will come to
Sheikh Jarrah, in East Jerusalem, to
stand with the helpless and despised

blocking the children of Israel from stealing their homes.
Over there, see my friends
Oscar Schindler and Abraham Joshua Heschel
chatting with some folks whose names you'd
never know, who rode the dangerous Greyhounds
through the South in 'sixty-one;
four years later, on Bloody Sunday, took a
beating in Selma, Alabama;
marched with Doctor King on Turnaround Tuesday
halfway across the Pettus Bridge;

braved the miles from Selma to Montgomery.
They called the kippot worn by Rabbis
in the march's vanguard 'freedom caps.'
Over there, playing croquet,
see my friends Elizabeth Cady Stanton,
Yasodhara, Prajapati,
Frederick Douglass, and Susan B. Anthony.
Nice shot, Susan! That man
whom you see retrieving the ball, his name was
stolen from him, boarding a ship; he

barely survived the voyage, or the years his
personhood was stolen from him;
in its place, he was allowed a subsistence
diet and made to dig with a hoe.
Harriet Tubman showed him the way to here.
On the day he first set foot in
Maryland, he reclaimed his full humanity,
named himself, and arrived at last."
"Is he, too, your friend?" I ask. The smile is
gracious. He says, "Yes, they all are.

That man he is greeting, with six dozen
kindred spirits, made Vermont the
New World's truest birthplace of freedom,
four score and six years
prior to Mister Lincoln's Proclamation.
Every summer solstice, they,
all Miz Tubman's hundreds of passengers, and the
Underground Railroad station keepers
gather underneath those trees at dusk, for a
fortnight of silent meditation.

Sometimes, Massasoit joins them. Over
there, he's throwing horseshoes with some
folks who, though they still can carve a turkey,
party here, after they've left
jugs of water and packets of food for migrants
trekking across the Sonoran Desert.
Have I answered your question? I could go on.
I would like to share a story
from the faith community you were born to
and its vernal feast of remembering

exile as homeless refugees in the desert.
In the scriptures that command this
celebration, scholars discovered four
different ways of describing the parents'
obligation to teach their children about it.
From this, they deduced that there are
four different kinds of children. Or, as
my friend Cheng Yi likes to say,
there's a single principle and a diversity
of particularizations.

Even in a dream, which this is not, you
cannot see or experience everything.
You are running out of time to be here.
Look! There, the two who saw what
kind of child you were, and taught you accordingly.
They have Something yet to show you,
if you don't lose time by getting lost in the
merely personal – a strong temptation! But,
goodness, what a loss! Please, allow me to
greet them on behalf of you."

Canto XXXIII: It's Like, You Know, Indescribable

Standing by, I listen as he tells my
parents what is needed and why,
using the simple eloquence a child might
patiently, gently use to explain a
mystery. Meanwhile, I indulge in just what
he had warned against, losing
not a second, losing only any
memory of his words, which anyway
weren't meant for me. I study my parents.
Mom, who's still disoriented

from her recent translation, embraces Dad as
if he replaces all she has lost, her
head resting against his shoulder, at ease.
Arms around her, solid, erect,
Dad looks straight at me, his face expressing
calm and relaxation. In life,
he withstood the strain of being what a
man of his generation expected his
wife to be, the family's emotional anchor,
in a manly way for a man of his

generation, that is, by not talking
of it, by not showing it, but
later rather than sooner bending if not
breaking under it, and softening
to the tender wisdom he took with him
out of our world, when he left.
Nothing if not steady, my Dad's level
gaze, and blue as the ocean's offing
on a cloudless August morning. Tilted
slightly from leaning on her husband, my

mother's honey brown, epicanthic
eyes convey alert intelligence
somewhat more complex and indirect.
His full lips are straight in repose
under his thick moustache, like a quiet
country lane beneath its trees.
Her lips are compressed in the trace of a smile,
Mona Lisa's, if she'd lived to
eighty and had seen a lot of pain.
Though politely giving Fred his

due attention, they beam straight at
me a love so fundamental
it's like drinking from a waterfall.
Fred's words trail off,
now unneeded. We know what to do.
Into this gusher that flows both ways, I
swim like a salmon, almost if not entirely
boggled at fitting what's happening into
something intelligible I can say to you.
Our language is insufficiently

synesthetic. No vocabulary
known to me, except perhaps the
technical terms invented by mystics and shamans,
inaccessible as the higher
mathematics to the rest of us,
tags what cannot be detected
by the five quotidian senses and the
gadgets we use to extend them.
Even that allusive and delicate mode of
intersubjectivity, poetry,

unsurpassable in its power to posit
with precision what can't be said,
never has evolved through thousands of years the
means to more than barely evoke,
much less closely and fully describe,
even in Rumi's dancing tropes,
such phenomena, so abnormal and alien.
But, I'll give it my best shot.
Every day, we see and hear and touch and
taste and smell and feel and dream of

numberless things for which we have no words.
Sometimes, words having failed us, we stammer,
like stroke victims who know exactly
what they want to say but, even
if their bodies could be persuaded to form the
sounds, they cannot locate the language.
Over those two facts, a bridge between us,
I will push my square-wheeled cart.
Scintillations shower around us. Now I
hear them loud as the voice you're hearing

in this ink, splashes of cacophony,
in which, slowly, I make out,
threading through them, ribbons of vocalise. I
think of Clare Torry soaring and
swooping through The Great Gig In The Sky.
Disentangling line from line, the
random barrage of din I'd thought I heard
breaks into a myriad voices;
but, don't be misled by "voices," they're neither
evanescent nor invisible.

Rather, I experience fluid fibres of
meanings beyond my ken; currents of
sentiments I can only guess at; colors
streaming through jillions of streams of
color; sound and light in dendritic profusion.
Those first songs I recognized, I
trace to my Mom and Dad, neither of whom could
carry a tune, but these are tunes no
larynx ever uttered, fine as the lines
drawn by magnetized iron shavings,

capillaries singing back and forth.
Fred says, "Wider." Click! My view
spraddles open, far to the sides and beyond.
Think of water jetting from a
garden hose, a sprinkler, or a fountain,
hanging motionless in midair, and
singing bursts from it like fragments of light.
Think of a sonorous, liquid network
we are strung on, ganglionic nodes that
send, receive, and shimmer, every

one a reservoir that spouts connection.
Now I see us, altogether submerged in a
heaving bath of our collective selves.
Now I see us, prodigiously ramified,
complex as a mycorrhizal mat,
stretching tendrils to the beach's
bordering fringe of trees, its grasses, crustaceans,
insects, weeds, and birds, and now, I
scry among them the palest scintillations,
bearing indescribable musics.

Fred says, "That's what Bach was listening to."
Shifting across the windless beach
filamentous mists bunch and thin.
We're as purposive and as brainless
as a shoal of minnows, a slime mold, a
forest, a beehive, a gannet colony.
I look down at my navel, bleeding colorful
trickles full of hallelujah
into the mighty, lustrous estuary.
Is that a tide of praise I hear?

I look over at Fred, limpid as if he were
born that way. Living people, to
whom the beach is just a beach, have brought their
bodies here, visible among the
ebbing and waxing, vapory bulges and swirls,
vaguely outlined, rapidly moving and
vanishing forms I find it hard to distinguish
one from another. "Isn't it silly,"
Fred says, "always to be looking for a
theory that ties it all together?

You, my friend, are the theory." He lays his hands
over my eyes as if we're playing a
children's game, but, through his fingers, I see
neither beach, nor sea, nor bodies,
only flawless cerulean with a cumulus
ceaselessly metamorphosing into
new forms of itself, inhabiting winds,
boiling with possibilities the
winds bring to it and take away.
Where the cloud is growing, droplets

crystallize, singing like bowls as they swell into being.
Inside every droplet something
flings its 'aye,' flitting from thing to thing,
seeking something to attach to,
finding nothing more substantial than rainbows.
Where the cloud's receding, it thins to
feathered flags. Crystals sublimate.
Droplets diminish, disappear; the
numinous strands come unknotted, loosing
singing – hear it! – even from the

Notes on the Text and Sources

No, the book isn't missing a page. That was the poem, finding the void.

In writing this book, and entirely without intending to, I seem to have followed Dante not only by borrowing his narrative structure, but also through the accretion of notes to the text. I hope my poem can be enjoyed without them, but that they will reward the curious reader.

The conceit of Dante's Paradiso is that he travels through the various heavenly spheres until he arrives at a vision of the final one, which both encompasses and lies at the center of everything else. Each sphere is associated with one of the planets known to Dante's time, or, after he gets beyond Saturn, with another heavenly characteristic. This schema tenuously informs my itinerary, without ever being directly alluded to. For what it may be worth, in Dante, the divisions fall as follows: EDEN, Canto I into Canto II; THE MOON, Canto II into Canto V; MERCURY, Canto V through Canto VII; VENUS, Canto VIII into Canto X; THE SUN, Canto X into Canto XIV; MARS, Canto XIV into Canto XVIII; Jupiter, Canto XVIII through Canto XX; SATURN, Canto XXI into Canto XXII; STARRY SPHERE, Canto XXII into Canto XXVII; CRYSTALLINE SPHERE , Canto XXVII through Canto XXIX; EMPYREAN, Canto XXX through Canto XXXIII.

Canto III

I owe a few words to Reuben Buckman Claflin, father of the once-famous stockbroker, Marxist revolutionary, woman suffragist, orator, free love advocate, spiritualist, newspaper publisher, and presidential candidate Victoria Woodhull. Readers familiar with her history may confuse him with the father of the woman who tells her story in Canto III. While Mr. Claflin was a vile man, capable of the most extreme cruelty and fraud in the cause of making a buck, the evidence that he sexually molested his daughters is sketchy, circumstantial, and ambiguous at best. The evidence that he pimped them out is somewhat stronger, but only somewhat. Only one of Ms. Woodhull's several biographers has embraced fully the charge that Buck was an incestuous paedophile. He is thus to be distinguished from the father of the woman in Canto III, for whose guilt of this crime the evidence is conclusive. That is to say: The present book is no more a history than it is a work of biography, philosophy, theology, autobiography, literary criticism, or journalism. It is a poem. Whatever truths it contains must be found within its four corners. Where they can be corroborated, so be it.

By the same token, I am happy to say that I am able to resolve a question that has plagued commentators on Dante's Commedia for seven hundred years. Did he actually experience the things that he describes in his books? The answer, I am pleased to tell you, is yes he did, and so have I.

Canto VII
"It is interesting to contemplate," etc. begins the last paragraph of Charles Darwin's On the Origin of Species.

Canto VIII
The quoted sonnet is my translation of Dante's sonnet to his friend Guido Cavalcanti, item number LII of the Rime in the Minor Works section of the Princeton Dante Project's invaluable website. The Princeton Dante Project also offers an English translation which is probably more accurate, strictly speaking, but I think mine is better poetry.

Paul, who makes his appearance in this canto, last was seen in Canto XXVII of To Join the Lost.

Canto IX
I am indebted to David Ferry for his translation of Gilgamesh (Farrar, Strauss & Giroux 1992).

Canto XI

"Presidential Library": See <u>Among the Lost</u>, Canto VIII.

Canto XII

Several lines are borrowed from the Autobiography of Eleanor Roosevelt with only slight modification, as I could not improve on the first lady's description of her youthful self except for purposes of prosody: "quiet conventional young society matron" and "orthodox standards of goodness."

"Presidential Library": See <u>Among the Lost</u>, Canto VIII. It's where former presidents make atonement.

Canto XIII

FDR's explanation of the reasons for his silence on the anti-lynching bill is taken from the excellent biography FDR by Jean Edward Smith (Random House 2008), pages 399-400, modified slightly to fit the poem's metrical scheme. The actual recipient of the quoted rationale was Walter White, secretary of the National Association for Advancement of Colored People, but there is no basis for assuming that FDR would not have said something similar to Eleanor.

Canto XIV

Jeanette Rankin's explanation of her vote to refrain from entering the First World War is only slightly paraphrased. Two and a half decades later, back in Congress for a second term (she lost her first seat due to redistricting), she did it again, casting the lone vote against declaring war on Japan, an act well described by a contemporary newspaper as having "stood firm in the folly of her faith."

Canto XV

"...up to your eyeballs in Anger...." See <u>To Join the Lost</u>, Canto VIII. The old unionist shares certain biographical details with my paternal grandfather. Those interested in historical reality may make a closer encounter with this amazing gentleman by accessing his unpublished autobiographical sketch among the Isidor Stenzor Collection in the Kheel Center for Labor-Management Documentation and Archives at the Cornell University Library. (It will be helpful to have some prior acquaintance with the history of the Communist Party and the United States labor movement in the first part of the twentieth century.) I have appropriated some of his phrases, i.e.. "stormy and interesting life," "miserable wages," "sweatshop conditions," and paraphrased some of his thoughts. Other thoughts expressed here probably never would have been expressed by the living Isidor Stenzor.

"Zaide" is Yiddish for "grandpa."

"Oy, dem epl iz farfoylt!" is Yiddish for "Oh, the apple is rotten!"

"Ven iz meyn nomen gevarn Itzkhok?" is Yiddish for "When did my name become Isaac?"

Canto XVI
"Alte kaker" is Yiddish for "old fart," literally "old shitter."

Canto XVII
"Meyn ainikle" is Yiddish for "my grandson."

"Nakhes" is Yiddish for the joy one takes in the accomplishments of another, reflected, as it were, back on oneself; e.g., a parent's pride in a child.

"Dayenu" is Hebrew for "it would have been enough." It also is the title and refrain of a song sung at Passover, expressing gratitude for the cascade of blessings the Jews experienced in connection with our liberation.

"Meyn foter" is Yiddish for "my father."

"Nu, farshteyst?" is Yiddish for "So, do you understand?"

"Gonif" is Yiddish for "thief."

"Paskudnyak" is Yiddish for someone who behaves in a nasty or contemptible manner, although to so define it is to minimize just how derogatory the term is.

Canto XVIII

"Goy" is a Yiddish term for a non-Jew. I regret to say that it has a more or less derogatory overtone. I am sure that the speaker used it purely out of habit, without intending any offence. This is heaven, after all.

Canto XIX

We saw Bunky last in To Join the Lost, Canto XXIX.

"Like this little fella's shadow rode you on his back, down there." See To Join the Lost, Canto VIII.

The exact wording of Genesis comes into question. Since Bunky's interlocutors have no Hebrew, except for the old unionist who retained a bit from his bar mitzvoh, Bunky is using the Everett Fox translation of Genesis 2:15-17, which Bunky partly paraphrases and, in pertinent part, quotes.

Canto XX

"Island Pond": In an early morning raid in 1984, police and social workers took 112 children from their homes in Island Pond, Vermont, on the basis of allegations of child abuse. The children's parents were members of a religious group that had moved to the area in 1977 and had neither been welcomed nor had sought to assimilate into this small, rural town. One of the group's tenets was "spare the rod and spoil the child." Its practice of corporal punishment contributed to the abuse allegations, which were never substantiated. The same day as the raid, Judge Mahady dismissed the State's warrants and petitions for lack of any constitutional basis and ordered the children returned to their homes

"State v. Keller": I quote the following from the Reporter's Notes to the State of Vermont Model Criminal Jury Instructions: "In the case known as the

'Trial of the Winooski 44,' the necessity defense was successfully invoked by protesters who had refused to leave Senator Stafford's office until he agreed to hold a public discussion about the government's involvement with the war in Nicaragua. The case is officially known as State v. Keller *et al.*, No. 1372-4-84 CnCr. Judge Frank Mahady instructed the jury that the State bore the burden of proving beyond a reasonable doubt that the necessity did not exist or apply. See the book Por Amor Al Pueblo: Not Guilty! (Front Porch Publishing 1986). Also see the article by Linda Vance, Esq., 'The Necessity Defense in Political Trials: An Appraisal,' which appeared in The Vermont Bar Journal & Law Digest, Vol. 12, No. 2, April 1986."

The extended quotation concluding the canto is from the peroration of Chief Justice Amestoy's opinion for the Court in Baker v. State, 170 Vt. 194, 744 A.2d 864 (1999). It is verbatim, except for two or three words that were changed to fit the meter.

The Italian at the very end is from Canto XX of Dante's Paradiso. I translate the full tercet roughly as, "And you, mortals, hold back from making judgments; even we, who see into God, don't yet know [who all of the Chosen are]".

Canto XXII
"Malakh-Hamoves" is Yiddish for "Angel of Death." As I was finishing writing the first stanza of this canto, in which the character introduces itself, I began to experience a transient ischemic attack. That experience in part informs what follows. Such are the risks and rewards of poetry.

Canto XXIV
The phrase "the psalmist sings past my hearing" is lifted from my poem "An Agnostic Reads the Book of Psalms", published in Many Mountains Moving, Volume V, Number 1. Dante recites his definition of "faith" from his Paradiso, Canto XXIV, lines 64-65, translation by Robert and Jean Hollander.

Canto XXV
Dante recites the definition of "the hope that brings true love to those on

earth" as handed down in his Paradiso, Canto XXV, lines 67-69, translation by Robert and Jean Hollander. "We are entitled to the struggle, never the fruits," paraphrases the Bhagavad Ghita.

Canto XXVI

The vivid image, "sitting in a metal barrel which somebody is constantly blasting with a sledgehammer" is Vadim Orlov's description of what it felt like in Submarine B-59 under assault. Savistsky's outburst is quoted from Orlov. Orlov was a communications/intelligence officer on the sub. We have his eyewitness account of what occurred there, but not Vasily Arkhipov's. Arkhipov died before the incident became public knowledge, of cancer that might have resulted from being irradiated during the accident on K-19. According to Arkhipov's wife, he did not like to talk about the Cuba mission and declined to say anything when she asked him about it. History has no record of what Arkhipov said to Savistsky to persuade him to surface the ship. Details of the conditions aboard B-59 are as described by Orlov, and extrapolated from the reminiscences of A.F. Dubivko, Captain of USSR Submarine B-36, sister ship to B-59 and a participant in the Cuba mission.

Canto XXVII

Dante quotes his Paradiso, Canto XXVII, lines, 64-66. I would translate them: "And you, my son, who, because of your mortal mass, must go back down again, open your mouth and don't keep to yourself [what I have given to you]." I didn't use a translation here because the Italian sounds so good and intimate. The "Holy! Holy!" could be a quote from many sources. Dante is thinking of Allen Ginsburg's great "Kaddish."

Canto XXIX

In light of Canto XXII's statement about the role poetry will take in our evolving understanding of the universe, I hasten to clarify that I have no pretensions to being the poet who will make such a contribution. Dante's fable is based on musings of my own, prompted by some recent works explaining for the lay public current thinking about particle physics and cosmology.

After indulging in these musings, I was delighted to discover that they are broadly consistent with a theory about the end of the universe called the Big Rip. The idea that the final dissolution will also constitute an act of creation is mine, although hardly original. I have no idea whether it comports with our current understanding of the behavior of quarks under these eschatological conditions, but I could not rid myself of the image of universes winking on all over, like Christmas tree lights, even as their parent universe goes dark.

"A kluger hert eyn vart, aun farshteyt tsvey" is a Yiddish proverb meaning "a wise man hears one word and understands two."

Canto XXXIII

"Clare Torry": the song is on Pink Floyd's great album, <u>Dark Side of the Moon</u>. Mary Pfahl also does a stellar job, on her remake of that record. It is her voice – not her speaking voice – that I hear behind the latter stanzas of this canto. I am indebted to Salman Rushdie's <u>Haroun and the Sea of Stories</u> for some of this canto's imagery.

Acknowledgments

Thanks to Samara Anderson, Esq., for help finding the light in Canto I; to beloved friend Susan Weiss, who, at the time of her death, was working on a novel about Eleanor Roosevelt, in which each chapter was about a different person, but all of them were Eleanor Roosevelt; to Valerie Koropatnik for the medallion and the book and all they betoken; to Joan Price and Kendra Holliday for steering me to Shamhat; to Marianne Vallet-Sandre for teaching me my first koans; to Rabbi Jan Salzman, an hour with whom opened so many windows; to Andrea Pappas; to Dr. Jennifer Spackman, for her love of words, her keen and appreciative eye, and her bold and sprightly spirit; to David Lustgarten, whose pamphlet, "A Book, A Building, and the Future of Our World" found me just as I was seeking inspiration for Canto XXIII; to Dr. Lisa Lax, Ed.D., for more than I can say here, not least including showing me David's pamphlet; to Marc Estrin and Donna Bister; and to the monthly poetry group hosted for so many years by Michael Beiner at the Flynndog (and elsewhere), at which *In Dante's Wake* was read in early drafts until the group's meetings were interrupted by the advent of the novel coronavirus around Canto XXIII of the present book. A writer must never, ever indulge in judging work in progress. It is paralyzing to do so. Unfortunately, that is the one thing a writer cannot help doing. Michael and the others gently and sweetly lifted me out of this dilemma time after time, bolstering my faltering courage with their unfailing acceptance. Blessings to all these people, and to those acknowledged in the previous books of this series, and most especially (in order of age) to Curt, Lise, Mira, and Isaac, with hugs and kisses. Last but the farthest possible from least, I give thanks to whoever or whatever used me as a vehicle for this work.

Fomite

More poetry from Fomite...

Anna Blackmer — *Hexagrams*
L. Brown — *Loopholes*
Sue D. Burton — *Little Steel*
David Cavanagh — *Cycling in Plato's Cave*
James Connolly — *Picking Up the Bodies*
Greg Delanty — *Loosestrife*
Mason Drukman — *Drawing on Life*
J. C. Ellefson — *Foreign Tales of Exemplum and Woe*
Tina Escaja/Mark Eisner — *Caida Libre/Free Fall*
Anna Faktorovich — *Improvisational Arguments*
Barry Goldensohn — *Snake in the Spine, Wolf in the Heart*
Barry Goldensohn — *The Hundred Yard Dash Man*
Barry Goldensohn — *The Listener Aspires to the Condition of Music*
R. L. Green — *When You Remember Deir Yassin*
Gail Holst-Warhaft — *Lucky Country*
Raymond Luczak — *A Babble of Objects*
Kate Magill — *Roadworthy Creature, Roadworthy Craft*
Tony Magistrale — *Entanglements*
Gary Mesick — *General Discharge*
Andreas Nolte — *Mascha: The Poems of Mascha Kaléko*
Sherry Olson — *Four-Way Stop*
Brett Ortler — *Lessons of the Dead*
David Polk — *Drinking the River*
Janice Miller Potter — *Meanwell*
Janice Miller Potter — *Thoreau's Umbrella*
Philip Ramp — *The Melancholy of a Life as the Joy of Living It Slowly Chills*
Joseph D. Reich — *A Case Study of Werewolves*
Joseph D. Reich — *Connecting the Dots to Shangrila*
Joseph D. Reich — *The Derivation of Cowboys and Indians*
Joseph D. Reich — *The Hole That Runs Through Utopia*
Joseph D. Reich — *The Housing Market*
Kenneth Rosen and Richard Wilson — *Gomorrah*
Fred Rosenblum — *Playing Chicken with an Iron Horse*
Fred Rosenblum — *Vietnumb *
David Schein — *My Murder and Other Local News*
Lawrence Schimel — *Desert Memory: Poems of Jeannette L. Clariond*
Harold Schweizer — *Miriam's Book*
Scott T. Starbuck — *Carbonfish Blues*
Scott T. Starbuck — *Hawk on Wire*
Scott T. Starbuck — *Industrial Oz*
Seth Steinzor — *Among the Lost*
Seth Steinzor — *To Join the Lost*

Fomite

Susan Thomas — *In the Sadness Museum*
Susan Thomas — *The Empty Notebook Interrogates Itself*
Sharon Webster — *Everyone Lives Here*
Tony Whedon — *The Tres Riches Heures*
Tony Whedon — *The Falkland Quartet*
Claire Zoghb — *Dispatches from Everest*

Poetry - Dual Language
Vito Bonito/Alison Grimaldi Donahue — *Soffiata Via/Blown Away*
Antonello Borra/Blossom Kirschenbaum — *Alfabestiario*
Antonello Borra/Blossom Kirschenbaum — *AlphaBetaBestiaro*
Antonello Borra/Anis Memon — *Fabbrica delle idee/The Factory of Ideas*
Aristea Papalexandrou/Philip Ramp — *Μας προσπερνά/It's Overtaking Us*
Mikis Theodoraksi/Gail Holst-Warhaft — *The House with the Scorpions*
Paolo Valesio/Todd Portnowitz — *La Mezzanotte di Spoleto/Midnight in Spoleto*

For more information or to order any of our books, visit:
http://www.fomitepress.com/our-books.html

Writing a review on Amazon, Good Reads, Shelfari, Library Thing or other social media sites for readers will help the progress of independent publishing. To submit a review, go to the book page on any of the sites and follow the links for reviews. Books from independent presses rely on reader-to-reader communications.

www.ingramcontent.com/pod-product-compliance
Lightning Source LLC
Chambersburg PA
CBHW030323100526
44592CB00010B/538